WITHDRAWN
BY
WILLIAMSBURG REGIONAL LIBRARY

JUN -- 2013

D1456294

Special Knits

Special Knits

22 Gorgeous Handknits for Babies and Toddlers

Debbie Bliss

WILLIAMSBURG REGIONAL LIBRARY
7770 CROAKER ROAD
WILLIAMSBURG, VIRGINIA 23188

Trafalgar Square Publishing

North Pomfret, Vermont

First published in the United States of America in 2005
by Trafalgar Square Publishing, North Pomfret, VT 05053

Copyright © Collins & Brown Limited 2005

Text copyright © Debbie Bliss 2005
Illustrations copyright © Collins & Brown 2005
Photographs copyright © Sandra Lousada 2005

**The designs in this book are copyright and
must not be knitted for resale.**

The right of Debbie Bliss to be identified as the author of
this work has been asserted by her in accordance with the
Copyright, Designs and Patents Act, 1988.

All rights reserved. No part of this publication may be
reproduced, stored in a retrieval system, or transmitted in
any form or by any means, electronic, mechanical,
photocopying, recording or otherwise, without the prior
written permission of the copyright owner.

1 3 5 7 9 8 6 4 2

Library of Congress Control Number
2004111233

ISBN 1 57076 296 1

Edited and designed by
Collins & Brown Limited

Editor: Kate Haxell
Designer: Roger Hammond
Photography: Sandra Lousada
Pattern checking: Rosy Tucker
Illustrations: Luise Roberts

Reproduction by Classicscan Pte Ltd

Printed in China

Contents

Introduction

Special Knits reflects our need to create beautiful handknits for babies in soft yarns that are gentle against delicate skin, each stitch invested with love and care by the knitter.

There are simple designs in this book where the special quality lies in the softness of the fabric, usually a cashmere mix. There are other projects where the uniqueness of the design comes from a scattering of beads, a velvet bow, or an organza ribbon that frames the gentle curve of a baby's cheek. In an age of the throwaway, these are garments that I hope will become the modern classic, knits to cherish and hand down through generations.

Most of the designs require little knowledge of complicated techniques; a simple garter-stitch blanket is perfect for a beginner and is given a touch of luxury with an edging of satin. Easy knits are embellished with decorative touches, while for those knitters who prefer more of a challenge, there is a sampler blanket or a cross-stitch embroidered gingham cardigan.

Debbie Bliss

eyelet vest

MEASUREMENTS

| To fit ages | | 6–12 | 12–18 | 18–24 | 24–36 | months |

ACTUAL MEASUREMENTS

| Chest | | 18½ | 20½ | 22 | 24 | in |
| Length to shoulder | | 11 | 12¼ | 13½ | 15¾ | in |

MATERIALS

• 2(3:3:4) 1¾oz (50g) balls Debbie Bliss baby cashmerino in Mallard
• Pair each of US 2 (2¾mm) and US 3 (3¼mm) knitting needles
• US 2 (2¾mm) circular knitting needle
• One button
• 1¼yd narrow ribbon

GAUGE

25 sts and 34 rows to 4in square over st st using
US 3 (3¼mm) needles.

ABBREVIATIONS

See page 121.

BACK

With US 2 (2¾mm) needles, cast on 81(89:97:105) sts.
K 3 rows.
Change to US 3 (3¼mm) needles.
Beg with a k row work in st st until back measures
6(6¾:8:9½)in from cast on edge, ending with a p row.
Dec row K1, [k2tog, yf, skpo] 20(22:24:26) times.
61(67:73:79) sts.
Next row P to end.
Next row K2(0:3:1), * p2, k3; rep from * to last
4(2:5:3) sts, p2, k2(0:3:1).
These 2 rows form the rib patt.
Cont straight until back measures 7(8:9:10½)in from
cast on edge, ending with a p row.
Shape armholes
Bind off 6 sts at beg of next 2 rows and 4 sts at beg of
foll 2 rows. 41(47:53:59) sts.
Dec one st at each end of the next and every foll alt
row until 31(37:43:49) sts rem.
P 1 row **.
Back opening
Next row Patt 14(17:20:23) sts, turn and work on
these sts for first side of back opening, leave rem sts
on a spare needle.
Next row Cast on 3 sts, k these 3 sts, then p to end.
Next row Patt to last 3 sts, k3.

Next row K3, p to end.
Rep the last 2 rows until back measures
10(11:12¼:14½)in from cast on edge, ending with
a p row.
Shape neck
Next row Patt to last 6(8:8:10) sts, leave these sts on a
holder, turn.
Dec one st at neck edge on every row until
5(7:9:11) sts rem.
Cont straight until back measures
11(12¼:13½:15¾)in from cast on edge, ending
with a p row.
Shape shoulder
Bind off.
With right side facing, rejoin yarn to rem sts on spare
needle, patt to end.
Next row P to last 3 sts, k3.
Next row K3, patt to end.
Rep the last 2 rows until back measures
10(11:12¼:14½)in from cast on edge, ending
with a p row.
Shape neck
Next row Patt 6(8:8:10) sts, leave these sts on a
holder, patt to end.
Dec one st at neck edge on every row until
5(7:9:11) sts rem.
Cont straight until back measures
11(12¼:13½:15¾)in from cast on edge, ending
with a p row.
Shape shoulder
Bind off.

eyelet vest

FRONT

Work as given for Back to **.

Shape neck

Next row Patt 11(13:15:17) sts, turn and work on these sts for first side of neck shaping, leave rem sts on a spare needle.

Dec 1 st at neck edge on every foll alt row until 5(7:9:11) sts rem.

Cont without further shaping until front measures same as Back to shoulder, ending at side edge.

Shape shoulder

Bind off.

With right side facing, slip center 9(11:13:15) sts onto a holder, rejoin yarn to rem sts on spare needle, patt to end.

Complete to match first side, reversing shaping.

NECKBAND

Join shoulder seams.

With right side facing and US 2 (2¾mm) circular needle, slip 6(8:8:10) sts from left back holder onto needle, pick up and k9 sts up left back neck to shoulder, 17(17:18:19) sts down left front neck, k across 9(11:13:15) sts from front neck holder, pick up and k17(17:18:19) sts up right front neck to shoulder, 9 sts down right back neck, then k across 6(8:8:10) sts from right back holder. 73(79:83:91) sts.

Work backwards and forwards in rows.

K 1 row.

Buttonhole row (right side) K1, yf, k2tog, k to end.

K 1 row.

Bind off.

ARMBANDS

With right side facing and US 2 (2¾mm) needles, pick up and k60(66:72:78) sts evenly around armhole edge.

K 3 rows.

Bind off.

TO FINISH

Join side and armband seams.

Lap button band behind buttonhole band and catch in place at center back. Sew on button. Thread ribbon through eyelets to tie at center front.

garter-stitch blanket

MEASUREMENTS
Approximately 21¾ x 29in

MATERIALS
• Six 1¾oz (50g) balls Debbie Bliss cashmerino aran in Pale Gray
• Pair of US 8 (5mm) knitting needles
• Approximately 3yd of 2-in wide satin ribbon

GAUGE
18 sts and 36 rows to 4in square over garter stitch using US 8 (5mm) needles.

ABBREVIATIONS
See page 121.

TO MAKE
With US 8 (5mm) needles, cast on 100 sts.
Work in garter stitch (k every row) until blanket measures 29in from cast on edge.
Bind off.

EDGING
Press the ribbon in half along its length. Fold the ribbon over the edge of the blanket and working one side at a time, hand-stitch the edge of the ribbon to the blanket, folding in extra ribbon at the corners to form miters. Fold under the end of the ribbon and slip stitch in place to neaten.

ribbed jacket

MEASUREMENTS

To fit ages		0–3	3–6	6–9	9–12	12–24	months

ACTUAL MEASUREMENTS

		0–3	3–6	6–9	9–12	12–24	
Chest		18	20	20¾	23½	25	in
Length to shoulder		9	9¾	11	11¾	12½	in
Sleeve length		4¼	5	6	6¾	8	in

MATERIALS

• 4(4:5:5:6) 1¾oz (50g) balls of Debbie Bliss cashmerino aran in Pale Pink
• Pair of US 8 (5mm) knitting needles
• Long circular US 7 (4½mm) and US 8 (5mm) knitting needles
• Optional decorative fastening

GAUGE

18 sts and 24 rows to 4in square over st st using US 8 (5mm) needles.

ABBREVIATIONS

See page 121.

BACK, FRONT AND SLEEVES

(worked in one piece)

With US 8 (5mm) needles, cast on 44(48:52:56:60) sts. Beg with a k row, work 32(34:38:40:44) rows in st st. Change to US 8 (5mm) circular needle.

Shape sleeves

Cast on 5(6:7:8:9) sts at beg of next 8 rows. 84(96:108:120:132) sts.
Work a further 16(18:22:24:26) rows.

Divide for fronts

Next row K34(40:45:51:56) sts, leave these sts on a spare needle, bind off next 16(16:18:18:20) sts, k to end.
Cont on last set of 34(40:45:51:56) sts only for left front.
Work a further 16(18:22:24:26) rows, so ending at sleeve edge.

Shape sleeve

Bind off 5(6:7:8:9) sts at beg of next and 3 foll alt rows. 14(16:17:19:20) sts.
Work 32(34:38:40:44) rows in st st.
Bind off.
With wrong side facing, rejoin yarn to rem sts on spare needle for right front, p to end.
Work a further 17(19:23:25:27) rows, so ending at sleeve edge.

Shape sleeve

Bind off 5(6:7:8:9) sts at beg of next and 3 foll alt rows. 14(16:17:19:20) sts.
Work 32(34:38:40:44) rows in st st.
Bind off.

EDGING

With right side facing and US 7 (4½mm) circular needle, pick up and k46(50:54:58:62) sts evenly up right front, 22(22:26:26:30) sts from back neck and 46(50:54:58:62) sts evenly down left front. 114(122:134:142:154) sts.
1st row (wrong side) P2, * k2, p2; rep from * to end.
2nd row K2, * p2, k2; rep from * to end.
Rep the last 2 rows for 3(3:3½:3½:4)in, ending with a 2nd row.
Bind off loosely but evenly in rib.

TO FINISH

Join side and sleeve seams.

ribbed jacket

hooded sweater

MEASUREMENTS

To fit ages		0–3	3–6	6–9	9–12	12–24	months

ACTUAL MEASUREMENTS

Chest		19	21	22½	24½	26	in
Length to shoulder		9½	10¼	11	11¾	13½	in
Sleeve length		5½	6¼	7	8	8¾	in

MATERIALS

• 4(4:5:5:6) 1¾oz (50g) balls of Debbie Bliss cashmerino aran in Pale Blue
• Pair of US 8 (5mm) knitting needles

GAUGE

18 sts and 24 rows to 4in square over st st using US 8 (5mm) needles.

ABBREVIATIONS

See page 121.

BACK

With US 8 (5mm) needles, cast on 46(50:54:58:62) sts. Beg with a k row work in st st until back measures 9½(10¼:11:11¾:13½)in from cast on edge, ending with a p row.

Shape shoulders

Bind off 13(14:15:16:17) sts at beg of next 2 rows. Bind off rem 20(22:24:26:28) sts.

FRONT

Work exactly as given for Back until 16 rows less than Back to shoulder have been worked.

Divide for front opening

Next row (right side) K23(25:27:29:31) sts, turn and work on these sts only for first side of front, leave rem sts on a spare needle.

Next row P to end.

Next row K21(23:25:27:29), m1, k2.

Next row P to end.

Next row K21(23:25:27:29), m1, k3.

Next row P to end.

Cont to inc one st as set on 5 foll right side rows. 30(32:34:36:38) sts.

P 1 row.

Shape shoulder

Next row (right side) Bind off 13(14:15:16:17) sts, k a further 7(8:9:10:11) sts, m1, k to end.

Next row P18(19:20:21:22) sts, leave these sts on a holder.

With right side facing, rejoin yarn to rem sts on spare needle, k to end.

Next row P to end.

Next row K2, m1, k 21(23:25:27:29) sts.

Next row P to end.

Next row K3, m1, k 21(23:25:27:29) sts.

Cont to inc one st as set on 6 foll right side rows. 31(33:35:37:39) sts.

Next row (wrong side) Bind off 13(14:15:16:17) sts, p to end.

hooded sweater

HOOD

Next row (right side) [K10, m1, k8(9:10:11:12)] across sts of right front, cast on 38(40:42:44:46) sts for back, then [k8(9:10:11:12), m1, k10] across sts of left front. 76(80:84:88:92) sts.

Beg with a p row, work a further 35(37:39:41:43) rows in st st.

Bind off.

SLEEVES

With US 8 (5mm) needles, cast on 30(32:34:36:38) sts.

Beg with a k row, work 8(8:10:10:12) rows in st st.

Inc row K3, m1, k to last 3 sts, m1, k3.

Beg with a p row, work 3 rows in st st.

Rep the last 4 rows until there are 42(46:50:54:58) sts.

Cont straight until sleeve measures 6¼(7:8:8¾:9½)in from cast on edge, ending with a p row.

Bind off.

TO FINISH

Join shoulder seams. With center of bound off edge of sleeve to shoulder, sew on sleeves. Join side and sleeve seams. With right sides together fold hood in half and join bound off edges. Join cast on edge of hood to bound off sts of back neck.

embroidered kimono

MEASUREMENTS

To fit ages		3–6		6–12		12–18		months

ACTUAL MEASUREMENTS

Chest		21¼		22¾		24		in
Length to shoulder		12½		13½		14		in
Sleeve length		6¼		7		8		in

MATERIALS

• 4(4:5) 1¾oz (50g) balls of Debbie Bliss cotton cashmere in Teal (M)
• One 1¾oz (50g) ball of Debbie Bliss cotton cashmere in Brown (C)
• Pair each of US 3 (3¼mm) and US 5 (3¾mm) knitting needles
• Odds and ends of pale blue and straw-colored embroidery thread
• Embroidery needle

GAUGE

22 sts and 30 rows to 4in square over st st using US 5 (3¾mm) needles.

ABBREVIATIONS

See page 121.

BACK

With US 3 (3¼mm) needles and C, cast on 72(76:80) sts.
K 3 rows.
Change to US 5 (3¾mm) needles and M.
Beg with a k row work in st st.
Work 8(10:12) rows.
Dec row K8, skpo, k to last 10 sts, k2tog, k8.
Work 9 rows in st st.
Rep the last 10 rows 3 times more and the dec row again. 62(66:70) sts.
Cont straight until back measures 8¼(8¾:9)in from cast on edge, ending with a p row.
Shape armholes
Bind off 5 sts at beg of next 2 rows. 52(56:60) sts.
Cont straight until back measures 12½(13½:14)in from cast on edge, ending with a p row.
Shape shoulders
Bind off 7(7:8) sts at beg of next 2 rows and 6(7:7) sts at beg of foll 2 rows.
Leave rem 26(28:30) sts on a holder.

LEFT FRONT

With US 3 (3¼mm) needles and C, cast on 58(60:62) sts.
K 3 rows.
Change to US 5 (3¾mm) needles and M.
Beg with a k row work in st st.
Work 8(10:12) rows.
Dec row K8, skpo, k to end.
Work 9 rows in st st.
Rep the last 10 rows 3 times more and the dec row again. 53(55:57) sts.
Cont straight until front measures 8¼(8¾:9)in from cast on edge, ending with a p row.
Shape armhole
Next row Bind off 5 sts, k to end. 48(50:52) sts.
P 1 row.
Shape neck
Next row K to last 8 sts, turn and leave these sts on a holder.
Next row Sl 1, p to end.
Next row K to last 6 sts, turn and leave these sts on the same holder.
Next row Sl 1, p to end.
Next row K to last 4 sts, turn and leave these sts on the same holder.
Next row Sl 1, p to end.
Next row K to last 2 sts, turn and leave these sts on the same holder.
Next row Sl 1, p to end.
Next row K to last 2 sts, k2tog.
Next row P2 tog, p to end.
Rep the last 2 rows until 13(14:15) sts rem.
Cont straight until front measures same as Back to

embroidered kimono

shoulder, ending at armhole edge.

Shape shoulder

Bind off 7(7:8) sts at beg of next row.

Work 1 row.

Bind off rem 6(7:7) sts.

RIGHT FRONT

With US 3 (3¼mm) needles and C, cast on
58(60:62) sts.

K 3 rows.

Change to US 5 (3¾mm) needles and M.

Beg with a k row work in st st.

Work 8(10:12) rows.

Dec row K to last 10 sts, k2tog, k8.

Work 9 rows in st st.

Rep the last 10 rows 3 times more and the dec row
again. 53(55:57) sts.

Cont straight until front measures 8¼(8¾:9)in from
cast on edge, ending with a k row.

Shape armhole

Next row Bind off 5 sts, p to end. 48(50:52) sts.

Next row K8 sts, leave these sts on a holder, k to end.

Next row P to last st, sl 1.

Next row K6 sts, leave these sts on the same holder,
k to end.

Next row P to last st, sl 1.

Next row K4 sts, leave these sts on the same holder,
k to end.

Next row P to last st, sl 1.

Next row K2 sts, leave these sts on the same holder,
k to end.

Next row P to last st, sl 1.

Next row Skpo, k to end.

Next row P to last 2 sts, p2tog tbl.

Rep the last 2 rows until 13(14:15) sts rem.

Cont straight until front measures same as Back to
shoulder, ending at armhole edge.

Shape shoulder

Bind off 7(7:8) sts at beg of next row.

Work 1 row.

Bind off rem 6(7:7) sts.

KEY

STRAIGHT STITCH IN
PALE BLUE OR STRAW

STRAIGHT STITCH IN C

CHAIN STITCH IN C

SLEEVES

With US 3 (3¼mm) needles and C, cast on
34(36:38) sts.
K 3 rows.
Change to US 5 (3¾mm) needles and M.
Beg with a k row, work in st st, inc one st at each end
of the 3rd and every foll 6th row until there are
48(52:56) sts.
Cont straight until sleeve measures 6¾(7:8)in from
cast on edge, mark each end of last row with a
colored thread.
Work a further ¾in, ending with a p row.
Bind off.

RIGHT FRONT EDGING

With right side facing, US 3 (3¼mm) needles and C,
pick up and k44(46:48) sts evenly along right front
straight edge.
K 3 rows.
Bind off.

LEFT FRONT EDGING

With right side facing, US 3 (3¼mm) needles and C,
pick up and k44(46:48) sts evenly along left front
straight edge.
K 3 rows.
Bind off.

NECKBAND AND COLLAR

Join shoulder seams.
With right side facing, US 3 (3¼mm) needles and C,
pick up and k3 sts across row ends of right front
band, k20 sts from right front holder, pick up and
k27(29:31) sts up right front neck, k across 26(28:30)
sts at back neck, pick up and k27(29:31) sts down
left front neck, k20 sts from left front holder, pick up
and k3 sts across row ends of left front band.
126(132:138) sts.
K 3 rows.
Next row Bind off 31(32:33) sts, k to last 31(32:33)
sts, bind off these sts.
With wrong side facing, rejoin yarn to rem 64(68:72)
sts, k to end.
Next row K2, skpo, k to last 4 sts, k2tog, k2.
Rep the last row 5 times more.
Bind off.

TO WORK EMBROIDERY

Using the diagram on page 25, work embroidered
flower heads scattered randomly over all garment
pieces. Work straight stitch petals with pale blue and
straw embroidery thread and short straight stitch
flower centers and lazy daisy sepals with C.

TO FINISH

Sew sleeves into armholes, with row ends above
colored threads sewn to bound off sts at underarm.
Join side and sleeve seams. Sew 11in of ribbon to end
of right neckband. Sew 11in of ribbon to left front
level with right front tie. Make a crochet chain on end
of left neckband and another on the inside of the right
front at end of bound off sts of the armhole shaping
to tie inside.

embroidered kimono

ribbon-edged cardigan

MEASUREMENTS

To fit ages		0–3	3–6	6–9	9–12	12–24	months

ACTUAL MEASUREMENTS

Chest		19	20½	22	23½	25¼	in
Length to shoulder		8¼	9½	10¼	11	12½	in
Sleeve length		5	6	6¾	7½	8¾	in

MATERIALS

- 2(3:3:4:4) 1¾oz (50g) balls of Debbie Bliss baby cashmerino in Pale Pink
- Pair each of US 2 (3mm) and US 3 (3¼mm) knitting needles
- 5(6:6:6:7) buttons
- ¾(⅞:⅞:1:1)yd ruffle-edged ribbon

GAUGE

25 sts and 34 rows to 4in square over st st using US 3 (3¼mm) needles.

ABBREVIATIONS

See page 121.

BACK

With US 2 (3mm) needles, cast on 62(67:72:77:82) sts.
K 5 rows.
Change to US 3 (3¼mm) needles.
Next row (right side) K3, * p1, k4; rep from * to last 4 sts, p1, k3.
Next row P to end.
These 2 rows form the patt and are rep throughout.
Cont in patt until back measures 8¼(9½:10¼:11:12½)in from cast on edge, ending with a p row.
Shape shoulders
Bind off 9(10:11:11:12) sts at beg of next 2 rows and 9(10:11:12:13) sts at beg of foll 2 rows.
Leave rem 26(27:28:31:32) sts on a spare needle.

LEFT FRONT

With US 2 (3mm) needles, cast on 35(37:40:42:45) sts.
K 5 rows.
Change to US 3 (3¼mm) needles.
Next row K3, * p1, k4; rep from * to last 7(9:7:9:7) sts, p1, k6(8:6:8:6).
Next row K5, p to end.
Rep the last 2 rows 22(27:32:32:39) times more.
Shape neck
Next row K to last 7(8:9:10:11) sts, leave these sts on a holder.

Dec one st at neck edge on every row until 18(20:22:23:25) sts rem.
Cont straight until front measures same as Back to shoulder, ending at armhole edge.
Shape shoulder
Bind off 9(10:11:11:12) sts at beg of next row.
Work 1 row.
Bind off rem 9(10:11:12:13) sts.

RIGHT FRONT

With US 2 (3mm) needles, cast on 35(37:40:42:45) sts.
K 3 rows.
Next row (buttonhole row) (right side) K1, k2tog, yf, k to end.
K 1 row.
Change to US 3 (3¼mm) needles.
Next row K6(8:6:8:6), * p1, k4; rep from * to last 4 sts, p1, k3.
Next row P to last 5 sts, k5.
Rep the last 2 rows 3(4:5:5:5) times more.
Next row (buttonhole row) K1, k2tog, yf, k3(5:3:5:3), * p1, k4; rep from * to last 4 sts, p1, k3.
Next row P to last 5 sts, k5.
Rep the last 10(12:14:14:14) rows 3(3:3:3:4) times more.
Next row K6(8:6:8:6), * p1, k4; rep from * to last 4 sts, p1, k3.
Next row P to last 5 sts, k5.
Rep the last 2 rows 2(3:4:4:4) times more.
Shape neck
Next row (right side) K7(8:9:10:11) sts, leave these 7(8:9:10:11) sts on a holder, k to end.
Dec one st at neck edge on every row until 18(20:22:23:25) sts rem.

ribbon-edged cardigan

Cont straight until front measures same as Back to shoulder, ending at armhole edge.

Shape shoulder

Bind off 9(10:11:11:12) sts at beg of next row.

Work 1 row.

Bind off rem 9(10:11:12:13) sts.

SLEEVES

With US 2 (3mm) needles, cast on 29(33:35:39:39) sts.

K 5 rows.

Change to US 3 (3¼mm) needles.

Next row K4(1:2:4:4), * p1, k4; rep from * to last 5(2:3:5:5) sts, p1, k4(1:2:4:4).

Next row P to end.

These 2 rows set the patt.

Cont in patt, **at the same time**, inc and work into patt

one st at each end of the next and every foll 4th row until there are 47(51:57:63:71) sts.

Cont straight until sleeve measures 5(6:6¾:7½:8¾)in from cast on edge, ending with a p row.

Bind off.

NECKBAND

Join shoulder seams.

With right side facing and US 2 (3mm) needles, slip 7(8:9:10:11) sts from right front neck holder onto a needle, pick up and k16(16:17:17:18) sts up right front neck, k26(27:28:31:32) sts from back neck holder, pick up and k16(16:17:17:18) sts down left front neck, k7(8:9:10:11) from left front holder. 72(75:80:85:90) sts.

K 1 row.

Next row (buttonhole row) K1, k2tog, yf, k to end.

K 3 rows.

Bind off.

TO FINISH

Matching center of bound off edge of sleeve to shoulder, sew on sleeves. Join side and sleeve seams. Sew on buttons. Sew ribbon behind buttonhole band and around neck edge.

rabbit

MEASUREMENTS
Approximately 11in, excluding ears

MATERIALS
• Two 1¾oz (50g) balls of Debbie Bliss cashmerino aran in Duck Egg
• Small amount of cream yarn for pom-pom tail
• Pair of US 3 (3¼mm) knitting needles
• Washable polyester toy stuffing
• Gray embroidery wool for features

GAUGE
23 sts and 32 rows to 4in square over st st using US 3 (3¼mm) needles.

ABBREVIATIONS
m1L = inserting left needle from the front, lift strand between sts and k into back of it so base of made st slants to the left.
m1R = inserting left needle from the back, lift strand between sts and k into front of it so base of made st slants to the right.
Also see page 121.

FACE

With US 3 (3¼mm) needles, cast on 9 sts.

1st row (right side) Kfb, k6, kfb, k1.

2nd row and every wrong side row P.

3rd row Kfb, k4, m1R, k1, m1L, k3, kfb, k1. 15 sts.

5th row Kfb, k6, m1R, k1, m1L, k5, kfb, k1. 19 sts.

7th row Kfb, k8, m1R, k1, m1L, k7, kfb, k1. 23 sts.

9th row Kfb, k9, m1R, k3, m1L, k8, kfb, k1. 27 sts.

11th row Kfb, k10, m1R, k5, m1L, k9, kfb, k1. 31 sts.

13th row K11, k2tog, k5, skpo, k11. 29 sts.

15th row K10, k2tog, k5, skpo, k10. 27 sts.

17th row K1, k2tog, k6, k2tog, k5, skpo, k6, skpo, k1. 23 sts.

19th row K1, k2tog, k4, k2tog, k5, skpo, k4, skpo, k1. 19 sts.

21st row K1, k2tog, k2, k2tog, k5, skpo, k2, skpo, k1. 15 sts.

23rd row K1, [k2tog] twice, k5, [skpo] twice, k1. 11 sts.

P 1 row.

Bind off.

BACK

Gusset

With US 3 (3¼mm) needles, cast on 22 sts.

Beg with a k row, work 6 rows in st st.

Cont in st st, dec one st at each end of next 8 rows. 6 sts.

Bind off.

Back

With right side facing, pick up and k42 sts around shaped edge of gusset.

Beg with a p row, work 15 rows in st st.

Dec row (right side) K1, [k2tog] 10 times, [skpo] 10 times, k1. 22 sts.

Beg with a p row, work 11 rows in st st.

Shape armholes

Bind off 2 sts at beg of next 2 rows. 18 sts.

Dec row (right side) K1, k2tog, k to last 3 sts, skpo, k1. 16 sts.

Work 5 rows in st st.

Shape shoulders

Bind off 3 sts at beg of next 2 rows. 10 sts.

Work 2 rows in st st.

Shape back of head

Inc row (right side) Kfb, k to last 2 sts, kfb, k1. 12 sts.

Cont in st st, inc in this way at each end of next 3 right side rows. 18 sts.

Work 5 rows in st st.

Dec one st at each end of next row and 4 foll right side rows. 8 sts.

Bind off.

FRONT

With US 3 (3¼mm) needles, cast on 22 sts.

Beg with a k row, work 16 rows in st st.

Dec one st at each end of next row. 20 sts.

Work 11 rows in st st.

Shape armholes

Bind off 2 sts at beg of next 2 rows. 16 sts.

Dec row (right side) K1, k2tog, k to last 3 sts, skpo, k1. 14 sts.

Work 5 rows in st st.

Shape shoulders

Bind off 2 sts at beg of next 2 rows. 10 sts.

34   r a b b i t

Dec row (right side) K1, k2tog, k to last 3 sts, skpo, k1. 8 sts.
Work 2 rows in st st.
Bind off.

LEGS

(make 2)
With US 3 (3¼mm) needles, cast on 5 sts.
1st row (right side) [Kfb] 4 times, k1. 9 sts.
P 1 row.
Inc one st at each end of next row and foll 2 right side rows. 15 sts.
Work 17 rows in st st **.
Shape thighs
1st row (right side) K6, [kfb] twice, k7. 17 sts.
Working one more st before and after incs, inc 2 sts in this way at center of next 5 right side rows. 27 sts.
Work 9 rows in st st.
Next row (right side) K11, skpo, k1, k2tog, k11. 25 sts.
P 1 row.
Next row (right side) K10, skpo, k1, k2tog, k10. 23 sts.
P 1 row.
Bind off.

ARMS

(make 2)
Work as given for Legs to **.
Shape top
Bind off 2 sts at beg of next 2 rows. 11 sts.
Dec one st at each end of next row. 9 sts.
P 1 row.
Bind off.

EARS

(make 2)
With US 3 (3¼mm) needles, cast on 7 sts.
1st row (right side) Kfb, k to last 2 sts, kfb, k1. 9 sts.
2nd row K1, p to last st, k1.
Cont in st st with k1 edge sts, inc one st at each end of next 3 right side rows. 15 sts.
Work 31 rows straight.
Dec row (right side) K2, skpo, k to last 4 sts, k2tog, k2. 13 sts.
Dec in this way at each end of next 2 right side rows. 9 sts.
Work 1 row.
Bind off.

TO FINISH

Join inside leg seams. Stuff legs. Flatten tops of legs and slip stitch closed. Join back to front at side seams. Sew legs to cast on edge of front, then to cast on edge of back. Join arm seams. Stuff arms. Stuff body to armholes. Join shoulders and set in arms. Add more stuffing to body through neck hole. Fold cast on edge of face in half and join for chin seam. Join face to back of head, leaving a gap at the top. Stuff face. Roll bound off edges of ears and set ears into gap at top of head, closing seam between ears. Add more stuffing to head. Join face to neck.

Using gray embroidery thread and face shaping as a guide to placing features, embroider nose, mouth and eyes, pulling thread through head to indent eyes slightly.

Make a pom-pom from cream yarn and sew on for tail.

alphabet sweater

MEASUREMENTS

To fit ages	3	6	12	24	months

ACTUAL MEASUREMENTS

Chest	21¼	23¼	25½	27¼	in
Length to shoulder	10½	11¾	13	14¾	in
Sleeve length	6¼	7½	8¾	9¾	in

MATERIALS

- 4(5:5:6) 1¾oz (50g) balls of Debbie Bliss cashmerino aran in Teal
- Pair each of US 3 (3¼mm), US 5 (3¾mm) and US 7 (4½mm) knitting needles
- Cable needle
- 3 buttons
- Contrast embroidery yarn

Shape neck

Next row (wrong side) Patt 19(19:22:25) turn and cont on these sts only, leave rem sts on spare needle.

Dec one st at neck edge on next 6 rows. 13(13:16:19) sts.

Patt 1(1:5:5) rows.

Bind off.

With right side facing, slip center 16(22:22:22) sts onto a holder, rejoin yarn to rem sts, patt to end. 19(19:22:25) sts.

Complete to match first side.

SLEEVES

With US 3 (3¼mm) needles, cast on 36(36:42:42) sts.

K 6 rows.

Change to US 5 (3¾mm) needles.

1st row (right side) P1, [k2, p1] 5(5:6:6) times, k4, [p1, k2] 5(5:6:6) times, p1.

This row sets patt to match Back.

Cont in patt, work 5 more rows.

Change to US 7 (4½mm) needles.

1st row (right side) P1, [T2R, p1] 5(5:6:6) times, C4B, [p1, T2L] 5(5:6:6) times, p1.

This row sets patt to match Back.

Cont in patt, work 5 more rows.

Inc and take into patt one st at each end of next row, then on 5(8:8:11) foll 4th rows. 48(54:60:66) sts.

Patt 11(7:15:11) rows.

Bind off.

NECKBAND

Join right shoulder seam and mark position of left shoulder on back edge. With right side facing and US 3 (3¼mm) needles, pick up and k10(10:13:13) sts down left front neck, patt 6(9:9:9), [k2tog] twice, patt 6(9:9:9) from front neck holder, pick up and k10(10:13:13) sts up right front neck and 27(33:33:33) sts across back neck to marker. 61(73:79:79) sts.

K 3 rows.

Next row (right side) P1, [k2, p1] to end.

Rib 6 more rows.

Next row (wrong side) P.

Work 4 more rows in st st.

Bind off knitwise.

SHOULDER EDGING

With right side facing and US 3 (3¼mm) needles, pick up and k17(17:25:25) sts across left front shoulder and neckband.

Bind off knitwise.

Make 3 button loops on edging.

TO FINISH

Join end of left shoulder. Set in sleeves, sewing row ends at top of sleeve to bound off sts at underarms. Join side and sleeve seams. Using alphabet chart from Sampler Blanket on page 86 and contrast yarn, embroider your chosen letter in the front diamond using cross stitch, adapting curlicues to fit. Sew buttons onto back left shoulder.

alphabet sweater

check and cross-stitch jacket

MEASUREMENTS

To fit ages	6	18	24	months

ACTUAL MEASUREMENTS

Chest	21¾	24½	27¼	in
Length	10¼	13	16½	in
Sleeve	6¾	9½	12¼	in

MATERIALS

• 2(3:4) 1¾oz (50g) balls of Debbie Bliss cotton cashmere in Cream (D) and one 1¾oz (50g) ball in each of Magenta (A), Pink (B), Lilac (C), Purple (E), Gray-blue (F) and Navy (G)

• Pair each of US 3 (3¼mm) and US 6 (4mm) knitting needles

• One button

• 1⅜yd narrow ribbon

GAUGE

23 sts and 28 rows to 4in square over eyelet, band and gingham patt using US 6 (4mm) needles.

ABBREVIATIONS

pfb = p into front and back of st.
wyab = with yarn at back of work.
wyif = with yarn in front of work.
Also see page 121.

NOTE

When counting rows, remember that each gingham band takes 16 rows to work, but it looks less because of the slipped stitches.

BACK AND FRONTS

With US 3 (3¼mm) needles and A, cast on 135(151:167) sts.

1st row (right side) P1, [k1, p1] to end.
Change to B.

2nd row K1, [p1, k1] to end.
These 2 rows form rib.
Rib 1 more row B, 2 rows C and 3 rows D **.

Next row Rib to end and dec one st in center of row. 134(150:166) sts.

Next row (wrong side) Rib 4, kfb and leave these 6 sts on a holder for button band, k to last 5 sts, turn and leave these 5 sts on a holder for buttonhole band. 124(140:156) sts.
Change to US 6 (4mm) needles.

1st row (right side) K.

2nd row P2, [yo, p2tog] to end.

3rd row K.

4th row (wrong side) Using US 3 (3¼mm) needles, k to end.
Change to US 6 (4mm) needles.

5th row K.

6th row P.

7th row K.

8th row P.

9th row Using US 3 (3¼mm) needles, p to end.
Change to US 6 (4mm) needles.

10th row P.

11th row With C, k3, [sl2 wyb, k2] to last st, k1.

12th row With E, sl3 wyif, [p2, sl2 wyif] to last st, sl1 wyif.

13th row With E, sl3 wyab, [k2, sl2 wyab] to last st, sl1.

14th row With C, p.

15th row With D, k3, [sl2 wyab, k2] to last st, k1.

16th row With D, p3, [sl2 wyif, p2] to last st, p1.

17th row With C, k.

18th row As 12th row.

19th row As 13th row.

20th row As 14th row.

21st row As 15th row.

22nd row As 16th row.

23rd row As 17th row.

24th row As 12th row.

25th row As 13th row.

26th row With C, p3, [sl2 wyif, p2] to last st, p1.
Cont in D.

27th row K.

28th row With US 3 (3¼mm) needles, k to end.
These 28 rows form the patt.
Using F for C and G for E on alternate bands of

check and cross-stitch jacket

check patt, work these 28 rows 0(1:2) times more, then work 1st to 9th rows again.

Divide for back and fronts

Next row (wrong side) With D, p27(31:35) for left front, bind off 6 sts, p until there are 58(66:74) sts on right needle after bind off sts, bind off 6 sts, p to end for right front.

Right front

Shape armhole

Cont in check patt and dec one st at beg of 4th row, then at armhole edge on 3 foll 3rd rows. 23(27:31) sts.

Patt 3 rows.

Leave sts on a holder.

Back

Shape armholes

With right side facing, rejoin yarn to center 58(66:74) sts, cont in check patt and dec one st at each end of 4th row and 3 foll 3rd rows. 50(58:66) sts.

Patt 3 rows.

Leave sts on a holder.

Left front

Shape armhole

With right side facing, rejoin yarn to rem 27(31:35) sts, cont in check patt and dec one st at end of 4th row, then at armhole edge on 3 foll 3rd rows. 23(27:31) sts.

Patt 3 rows.

Leave sts on a holder.

SLEEVES

With US 3 (3¼mm) needles and A, cast on 41(45:49) sts.

Work as given for Back and Fronts to **.

Rib 1 more row D.

Cont in D.

Next row (wrong side) K.

Change to US 6 (4mm) needles.

1st row (right side) K.

2nd row P1, [yo, p2tog] to end.

3rd row K.

4th row Using US 3 (3¼mm) needles, k to end. Change to US 6 (4mm) needles.

5th row K.

6th row P.

7th row K to last 2 sts, kfb, k1. 42(46:50) sts.

8th row P.

9th row Using US 3 (3¼mm) needles, p to end. Change to US 6 (4mm) needles.

10th row P.

11th row With C, k2, [sl2 wyb, k2] to end.

12th row With E, sl2 wyif, [p2, sl2 wyif] to end.

13th row With E, sl2 wyab, [k2, sl2 wyab] to end.

14th row With C, p.

15th row With D, k2, [sl2 wyab, k2] to end.

16th row With D, p2, [sl2 wyif, p2] to end.

17th row With C, kfb, k to last 2 sts, kfb, k1. 44(48:52) sts.

18th row With E, sl3 wyif, [p2, sl2 wyif] to last st, sl1 wyif.

19th row With E, sl3 wyab, [k2, sl2 wyab] to last st, sl1 wyab.

20th row With C, p.

21st row With D, k3, [sl2 wyab, k2] to last st, k1.

22nd row With D, p3, [sl2 wyif, p2] to last st, p1.

23rd row With C, kfb, k to last 2 sts, kfb, k1. 46(50:54) sts.

24th row With E, p2, [sl2 wyif, p2] to end.

25th row With E, k2, [sl2 wyab, k2] to end.

26th row With C, sl2 wyif, [p2, sl2 wyif] to end. Cont in D.

27th and 28th rows K.

Using F for C and G for E on alternate bands of check patt and ending the 2nd patt row p1, work

these 28 rows 0(1:2) times more, omitting incs, then work 1st to 8th rows.

Shape top

Cont in patt in D and bind off 4 sts at beg of next 2 rows.

Cont in check patt, beg k2 F(C:F), dec one st at each end of 4th row and 3 foll 3rd rows. 30(34:38) sts.

Patt 3 rows.

Leave sts on a holder.

YOKE

Joining row With right side facing, US 6 (4mm) needles and D, work [k21(25:29), skpo] across right front sts, [k2tog, k26(30:34), skpo] across right sleeve sts, [k2tog, k46(54:62), skpo] across back sts, [k2tog, k26(30:34), skpo] across left sleeve sts, then work [k2tog, k21(25:29)]across left front sts. 148(172:196) sts.

K 1 row.

1st dec row (right side) K2(1:2), [k2tog, k14(13:12), skpo] 8(10:12) times, k2(1:2). 132(152:172) sts.

Patt 3 rows.

2nd dec row (right side) K1, [k2tog, k6, skpo] 13(15:17) times, k1. 106(122:138) sts.

K 1 row.

3rd dec row (right side) K1, [k2tog, k4, skpo] 13(15:17) times, k1.

80(92:104) sts.

Patt 21 rows, so ending k 1 row D.

Cont in D.

4th dec row (right side) K1, [k2tog, k2, skpo] 13(15:17) times, k1.

54(62:70) sts.

check and cross-stitch jacket

Patt 3(3:9) rows.
Leave sts on a holder.

BUTTON BAND

With right side facing, US 3 (3¼mm) needles and D,
rib 6 sts from left front holder.
Cont in rib until band, when slightly stretched fits up
front edge to neck.
Leave sts on a holder.
Sew on band.
Place a marker for button 2in down from neck edge.

BUTTONHOLE BAND

With wrong side facing, US 3 (3¼mm) needles and D,
cast on one st, rib 5 sts from right front holder. 6 sts.
Cont to match button band, making buttonhole
opposite marker as folls:
Buttonhole row (right side) P1, k1, yo, k2tog, p1, k1.

NECKBAND

With right side facing, US 3 (3¼mm) needles and D,
beg at right front, [p1, k1] twice, p2tog from
buttonhole band holder, work [k1, p1] to last 2 sts,
skpo, from yoke holder, then work p2tog, [k1, p1]
twice from buttonband holder. 63(71:79) sts.
1st row (wrong side) P2, [k1, p1] to last st, p1.
Rib 1 more row D, 2 rows B and 1 row A.
With A, bind off in rib.

RIGHT FRONT EDGING

With US 3 (3¼mm) needles and B, beg and end with
B rows at lower edge and neck, pick up and
k55(71:93) sts up right front edge.

Beg k1, rib 1 row.
Change to A and rib 1 row.
Bind off purlwise.

LEFT FRONT EDGING

Work as Right Front Edging, on left front edge.

WORK EMBROIDERY

Work large cross stitches on alternate stockinette stitch
bands using A and pairs of chain stitches using B.

TO FINISH

Join underarm and sleeve seams. Join ends of front
edgings. Slot ribbon through eyelet holes on yoke and
secure ends. Sew on button.

ribbon-tied dress

MEASUREMENTS

| To fit ages | | 3–6 | | 6–12 | 12–18 | | 18–24 | | months |

ACTUAL MEASUREMENTS

Chest		19¾		22		24½		26½		in
Length to shoulder		14½		17¼		19		20½		in
Sleeve length		6		7		8		8¾		in

MATERIALS

- 4(5:5:6) 1¾oz (50g) balls Debbie Bliss baby cashmerino in White
- Pair each of US 2 (3mm) and US 3 (3¼mm) knitting needles
- 1¾yd ribbon

GAUGE

25 sts and 34 rows to 4in square over st st using US 3 (3¼mm) needles.

ABBREVIATIONS

See page 121.

BACK

With US 2 (3mm) needles, cast on 96(103:112:121) sts.

K 3 rows.

Change to US 3 (3¼mm) needles.

Beg with a k row work 6 rows in st st.

Dec row K12(13:14:15), skpo, k to last 14(15:16:17) sts, k2tog, k12(13:14:15).

Work 7(9:9:9) rows in st st.

Rep the last 8(10:10:10) rows 9(9:10:11) times more. 76(83:90:97) sts.

Cont straight until back measures 9¾(12¼:13½:14½)in from cast on edge, ending with a right side row.

Dec row P5, [p2tog, p5] 9(10:11:12) times, p2tog, p6. 66(72:78:84) sts. **

Cont straight until back measures 11(13½:14½:15¾)in from cast on edge, ending with a p row.

Shape armholes

Bind off 8(9:10:11) sts at beg of next 2 rows. 50(54:58:62) sts.

Cont straight until back measures 14½(17¼:19:20½)in from cast on edge, ending with a p row.

Shape shoulders

Bind off 10(11:12:13) sts at beg of next 2 rows.

Bind off rem 30(32:34:36) sts.

FRONT

Work as given for Back to **

Divide for front opening

Next row (right side) K24(26:28:30), turn and work on these sts for first side of neck, leave rem sts on a spare needle.

Next row Cast on 18(20:22:24) sts, k3, p2tog, p to end. 41(45:49:53) sts.

Next row K to last 4 sts, k2tog, k2.

Next row K3, p2tog, p to end.

Rep the last 2 rows 3 times more.

Shape armhole

Next row Bind off 8(9:10:11) sts, k to last 4 sts, k2tog, k2.

Next row K3, p to end.

Next row K to last 4 sts, k2tog, k2.

Cont to dec at neck edge on every alt row until 13(14:15:16) sts rem.

Cont without further shaping until front measures same as Back to shoulder, ending at armhole edge.

Shape shoulder

Bind off 10(11:12:13) sts at beg of next row.

Cont in garter st on rem 3 sts until band fits halfway across back neck.

Bind off.

With right side facing, rejoin yarn to rem sts, k18(20:22:24) sts, turn and work on these sts only.

Next row K1, p to last 5 sts, p2tog tbl, k3.

Next row K2, skpo, k to end.

Leave these sts on a spare needle.

Rejoin yarn to rem 24(26:28:30) sts, k to end.

Next row P to last st, k1.

Next row K to end.

ribbon-tied dress

Next row P to end, then work across sts on spare needle as folls: p to last 5 sts, p2tog tbl, k3. Complete to match first side.

SLEEVES

With US 2 (3mm) needles, cast on 36(38:42:46) sts.
K 5 rows.
Change to US 3 (3¼mm) needles.
Beg with a k row work in st st and inc one st at each end of the 3rd and every foll 6th row until there are 50(56:60:66) sts.
Cont straight until sleeve measures 6(7:8:8¾)in from cast on edge, ending with a p row.
Mark each end of last row then work a further 6(6:8:8) rows.
Bind off.

TO FINISH

Join bound off edges of 3-st band, sew to back neck edge. With center of bound off edge of sleeve to shoulder, sew sleeves into armholes with row ends above markers sewn to bound off sts at underarm. Sew cast on sts of left front behind right front. Join side and sleeve seams. Cut ribbon in half. Sew one end of each length to front edges. Thread left front ribbon through eyelet, take both ribbons around the back and bring forward to tie at center front.

shawl

MEASUREMENTS
Approximately 27¼ x 28¼in

MATERIALS
• Six 1¾oz (50g) balls of Debbie Bliss baby cashmerino in Pale Blue
• Pair of US 3 (3¼mm) knitting needles

GAUGE

25 sts and 34 rows to 4in square over st st using US 3 (3¼mm) needles.

ABBREVIATIONS

See page 121.

CENTRAL SQUARE

With US 3 (3¼mm) needles, cast on 159 sts.

Seed st row K1, [p1, k1] to end.

Rep this row 3 times more.

5th row (right side) [K1, p1] 4 times, * k3, [p1, k1] 3 times, p1; rep from * to last 11 sts, k3, [p1, k1] 4 times.

6th row (wrong side) [K1, p1] 3 times, k1, * p5, [k1, p1] twice, k1; rep from * to last 12 sts, p5, [k1, p1] 3 times, k1.

7th row [K1, p1] 3 times, * k7, p1, k1, p1; rep from * to last 3 sts, k1, p1, k1.

8th row [K1, p1] twice, k1, * p9, k1; rep from * to last 4 sts, [p1, k1] twice.

9th row [K1, p1] twice, k to last 4 sts, [p1, k1] twice.

10th row K1, p1, k1, p to last 3 sts, k1, p1, k1.

11th row As 9th row.

12th row [K1, p1] twice, k1, p to last 5 sts, [k1, p1] twice, k1.

13th row [K1, p1] 3 times, k to last 6 sts, [p1, k1] 3 times.

14th row [K1, p1] 3 times, k1, * p7, k1, p2; rep from * to last 12 sts, p5, [k1, p1] 3 times, k1.

15th row [K1, p1] 4 times, * k5, p1, k1, p1, k2; rep from * to last 11 sts, k3, [p1, k1] 4 times.

16th row As 14th row.

17th row As 13th row.

18th row As 12th row.

19th row As 9th row.

20th row As 10th row.

21st row As 9th row.

22nd row As 12th row.

23rd row As 13th row.

24th row [K1, p1] 3 times, k1, p12, * k1, p9; rep from * to last 10 sts, p3, [k1, p1] 3 times, k1.

25th row [K1, p1] 4 times, k10, * p1, k1, p1, k7; rep from * to last 11 sts, k3, [p1, k1] 4 times.

26th row As 24th row.

27th row As 13th row.

28th row As 12th row.

The last 20 rows (9th to 28th patt rows) form the patt and are repeated 9 times more.

Now work a further 11 rows, so ending with a 19th patt row.

Next 8 rows Work 8th, 7th, 6th, 5th, 4th, 3rd, 2nd, and 1st rows.

Bind off knitwise.

shawl

EDGING

With US 3 (3¼mm)needles, cast on 6 sts.

1st row K2, yf, k2tog, yf, k to end.

2nd row K all sts.

3rd to 13th rows Rep 1st and 2nd rows 5 times more, then the 1st row again. 13 sts.

14th row Bind off 7 sts, k to end. 6 sts.

These 14 rows form the edging patt and are repeated until straight edge fits all around the shawl edge, ending with a 13th row. Slip stitch edging in place to edge of shawl in short sections as you knit, easing to fit around the corners. Bind off all sts.

picot dress and bag

MEASUREMENTS

To fit ages	3–6	9–12	12–18	18–24	months

ACTUAL MEASUREMENTS

Chest	18½	20½	22	24	in
Length to shoulder	14	16	19¼	21¾	in

MATERIALS

• Dress: 4(5:6:7) 1¾oz (50g) balls Debbie Bliss baby cashmerino in Lilac
• Bag: One 1¾oz (50g) ball Debbie Bliss baby cashmerino in Lilac
• Pair each of US 2 (2¾mm) and US 3 (3¼mm) knitting needles
• US 2 (2¾mm) circular knitting needle
• 1 button
• 12in of narrow ribbon for dress and 1¾yd narrow ribbon for bag

GAUGE

25 sts and 34 rows to 4in square over st st using US 3 (3¼mm) needles.

ABBREVIATIONS

ssk = [slip 1 knitwise] twice, insert tip of left needle into fronts of slipped sts and k2tog.
kp = knit and purl into next st.
pk = purl and knit into next st.
Also see page 121.

DRESS BACK

** With US 3 (3¼mm) needles, cast on 101(109:117:125) sts.

Seed st row K1, [p1, k1] to end.

Rep this row 5 times more.

Beg with a k row work 6 rows in st st.

Dec row (right side) K10(11:12:13), ssk, k to last 12(13:14:15) sts, k2tog, k10(11:12:13).

Work 5(7:9:11) rows in st st.

Rep the last 6(8:10:12) rows until 81(89:97:105) sts rem.

Cont straight until back measures 9(10½:13½:15¼)in from cast on edge, ending with a p row.

Dec row K1, [k2tog, k2] 20(22:24:26) times. 61(67:73:79) sts.

Seed st row K1, [p1, k1] to end.

Cont straight in seed st until back measures 10¼(11¾:14½:16½)in from cast on edge, ending with a wrong side row.

Shape armholes

Bind off 6 sts at beg of next 2 rows and 4 sts at beg of foll 2 rows.

Dec one st at each end of the next and every foll alt row until 31(37:43:49) sts rem.

Seed st 1 row. **

Back opening

Next row Seed st 14(17:20:23) sts, turn and work on these sts for first side of back opening.

Next row Cast on 3 sts, seed st these 3 sts, then seed st to end.

Cont in seed st until back measures 13(15:18:20½)in from cast on edge, ending with a wrong side row.

Shape neck

Next row Seed st to last 6(8:8:10) sts, leave these sts on a holder, turn.

Dec one st at neck edge on every row until 5(7:9:11) sts rem.

Cont straight until back measures 14¼(16:19¼:21¾)in from cast on edge, ending with a wrong side row.

Shape shoulder

Bind off.

With right side facing, rejoin yarn to rem sts, seed st to end.

Cont in seed st until back measures 13(15:18:20½)in from cast on edge, ending with a wrong side row.

Shape neck

Next row Seed st 6(8:8:10) sts, leave these sts on a holder, seed st to end.

Dec one st at neck edge on every row until 5(7:9:11) sts rem.

Cont straight until back measures 14¼(16:19¼:21¾)in from cast on edge, ending with a wrong side row.

Shape shoulder

Bind off.

DRESS FRONT

Work as given for Back from ** to **

Shape neck

Next row (right side) Seed st 11(13:15:17) sts, turn and work on these sts for first side of neck shaping.

Dec 1 st at neck edge on every foll alt row until 5(7:9:11) sts rem.

Cont without further shaping until front measures same as Back to shoulder, ending at side edge.

picot dress and bag

Shape shoulder
Bind off.
With right side facing, slip center 9(11:13:15) sts onto a holder, rejoin yarn to rem sts, seed st to end.
Complete to match first side, reversing shaping.

NECKBAND
Join shoulder seams.
With right side facing and US 2 (2¾mm) circular knitting needle, slip 6(8:8:10) sts from left back onto needle, pick up and k11 sts up left back to shoulder, 18(20:22:24) sts down left front neck, k across 9(11:13:15) sts from front neck holder, pick up and k18(20: 22:24) sts up right front neck to shoulder, 11 sts from right back neck, k across 6(8:8:10) sts on back neck holder. 79(89:95:105) sts.
Work backwards and forwards in rows.
K 1 row.
Buttonhole row K1, yf, k2tog, k to end.
Picot bind off row (wrong side) Working knitwise, bind off 5, * slip st from right needle back onto left needle, cast on 2 sts, bind off 5; rep from * ending last repeat: bind off rem sts.

ARMBANDS
Join left shoulder and neckband seam.
With right side facing and US 2 (2¾mm) knitting needles, pick up and k66(72:78:84) sts evenly around armhole edge.
K 2 rows.

Picot bind off row (wrong side) Working knitwise, bind off 12, [sl st from right needle back onto left needle, cast on 2 sts, bind off 5 sts] 15(17:19:21) times, bind off rem sts.

POCKET
With US 3 (3¼mm) needles, cast on 11 sts.
1st row K1, [p1, k1] to end.
2nd row As 1st row.
3rd row Pk, [p1, k1] to last 2 sts, p1, kp.
4th row P1, [k1, p1] to end.
5th row Kp, [k1, p1] to last 2 sts, k1, pk.
6th row K1, [p1, k1] to end.
Rep the last 4 rows 4 times more. 31 sts.
Work 6th row twice more.
Eyelet row (right side) K1, [p2tog, yo, p1, k2tog, yf, k1] twice, p2tog, yo, p1, yo, p2tog, [k1, yf, k2tog, p1, yo, p2tog] twice, k1.
Next row K1, [p1, k1] to end.
Picot bind off row (right side) Bind off 3, * sl st from right needle back onto left needle, cast on 2 sts, bind off 5 sts; rep from * to end.

TO FINISH
Join side and armband seams. Lap buttonband behind buttonhole band and catch in place. Sew on button. Cut ribbon in half and stitch one end of each length to wrong side of eyelet row ends of pocket. Thread ribbons through eyelets, pull up and tie at center front. Position pocket on dress front and slipstitch in place.

velvet-edged jacket

MEASUREMENTS

To fit ages		0–3	3–6	6–9	9–12	12–24	months

ACTUAL MEASUREMENTS

Chest		19	20½	22	23½	25½	in
Length to shoulder		8¼	9½	10¼	11	12½	in
Sleeve length		5	6	6¾	7½	8½	in

MATERIALS

- 2(3:3:4:4) 1¾oz (50g) balls of Debbie Bliss baby cashmerino in Pale Blue
- Pair each of US 2 (3mm) and US 3 (3¼mm) knitting needles
- 1¼yd narrow piped ribbon for edging
- 6(6:6:6:7) buttons

GAUGE

25 sts and 34 rows to 4in square over st st using US 3 (3¼mm) needles.

ABBREVIATIONS

See page 121.

BACK

With US 2 (3mm) needles, cast on 62(66:70:74:82) sts.
K 3 rows.
Change to US 3 (3¼mm) needles.
Beg with a k row, work in st st until back measures 4¾(5½:6:6¼:7)in from cast on edge, ending with a p row.

Shape armholes

Bind off 3(3:3:3:4) sts at beg of next 2 rows.
Dec one st at each end of the next and 3(3:3:3:4) foll alt rows. 48(52:56:60:64) sts.
Cont in st st until back measures 8¼(9½:10¼:11:12½)in from cast on edge, ending with a p row.

Shape shoulders

Bind off 13(14:15:16:17) sts at beg of next 2 rows.
Bind off rem 22(24:26:28:30) sts.

LEFT FRONT

With US 2 (3mm) needles, cast on 31(33:35:37:41) sts.
K 3 rows.
Change to US 3 (3¼mm) needles.
Beg with a k row, work in st st until front measures 4¾(5½:6:6¼:7)in from cast on edge, ending with a p row.

Shape armhole

Bind off 3(3:3:3:4) sts at beg of next row.
Work 1 row.
Dec one st at beg of the next and 3(3:3:3:4) foll alt rows. 24(26:28:30:32) sts.
Cont in st st until front measures 6¾(7½:8¼:8¾:10¼)in from cast on edge, ending with a p row.

Shape neck

Next row K to last 4(5:5:5:6) sts, leave these sts on a holder.
Dec one st at neck edge on every row until 13(14:15:16:17) sts rem.
Cont straight until front measures same as Back to shoulder, ending at armhole edge.

Shape shoulder

Bind off.

velvet-edged jacket

RIGHT FRONT

With US 2 (3mm) needles, cast on 31(33:35:37:41) sts.
K 3 rows.
Change to US 3 (3¼mm) needles.
Beg with a k row, work in st st until front measures
4¾(5½:6:6¼:7)in from cast on edge, ending with a
k row.

Shape armhole

Bind off 3(3:3:3:4) sts at beg of next row.
Dec one st at end of the next and 3(3:3:3:4) foll alt
rows. 24(26:28:30:32) sts.
Cont in st st until front measures
6¾(7½:8¼:8¾:10¼)in from cast on edge,
ending with a p row.

Shape neck

Next row K4(5:5:5:6) sts, leave these sts on a holder,
k to end.
Dec one st at neck edge on every row until
13(14:15:16:17) sts rem.
Cont straight until front measures same as Back to
shoulder, ending at armhole edge.

Shape shoulder

Bind off.

SLEEVES

With US 2 (3mm) needles, cast on 32(34:38:40:44) sts.
K 3 rows.
Change to US 3 (3¼mm) needles.
Beg with a k row, work in st st and inc one st at each
end of the 3rd and every foll 4th row until there are
50(54:60:66:74) sts.
Cont straight until sleeve measures
5¼(6:6¾:7½:8¾)in from cast on edge,
ending with a p row.
Bind off 3(3:3:3:4) sts at beg of next 2 rows.
Dec one st at each end of the next and 3(3:3:3:4) foll
alt rows. 36(40:46:52:56) sts.
Bind off.

BUTTON BAND

With right side facing and US 2 (3mm) needles,
leaving a long yarn end, pick up and k46(51:58:63:69)
sts along left front edge.
K 4 rows.
Bind off.

BUTTONHOLE BAND

With right side facing and US 2 (3mm) needles, pick up and k46(51:58:63:69) sts along right front edge.
K 1 row.
Buttonhole row (right side) K2(2:3:3:4), [k2tog, yf, k6(7:8:9:8) sts] 5(5:5:5:6) times, k2tog, yf, k2(2:3:3:3).
K 1 row.
Bind off.

COLLAR

Join shoulder seams.
With right side facing and US 3 (3¼mm) needles, slip 4(5:5:5:6) sts on right front holder onto a needle, pick up and k16(16:17:18:18) sts up right front neck, 22(24:26:28:30) sts from back neck and 16(16:17:18:18) sts down left front neck, then k4(5:5:5:6) sts from left front holder.
62(66:70:74:78) sts.
Beg with a k row work in st st, shaping as folls:
Next 2 rows Work to last 20(21:22:23:24) sts, turn.
Next 2 rows Work to last 14(15:16:17:18) sts, turn.
Next 2 rows Work to last 8(9:10:11:12) sts, turn.
Next row K all sts.
Next row P all sts.
Next row K1, m1, k to last st, m1, k1.
Next row P to end.
Rep the last 2 rows 3(4:4:5:5) times more.
70(76:80:86:90) sts.

Next row Skpo, k to last 2 sts, k2tog.
Next row P2tog, p to last 2 sts, p2tog tbl.
Rep the last 2 rows 1(2:2:3:3) times more.
With right side of collar facing, US 3 (3¼mm) needle and long yarn end from button band, pick up and k14(18:18:22:22) sts along row ends of collar, then using main ball of yarn k across 62(64:68:70:74) sts of collar, then pick up and k14(18:18:22:22) sts along row ends of collar. 90(100:104:114:118) sts.
Bind off knitwise.

TO FINISH

With center of bound off edge of sleeve to shoulder, sew sleeves into armholes. Join side and sleeve seams. Sew fabric edge of piped edging under the outside edge of collar, behind the buttonhole band and lower sleeve edges. Sew on buttons.

velvet-edged jacket

fair isle top

MEASUREMENTS

To fit ages		6–12		12–18	18–24		months

ACTUAL MEASUREMENTS

Chest		20½		22		24		in
Length to shoulder		11		12½		14		in
Sleeve length		7		7¼		9½		in

MATERIALS

- 3(3:4) 1¾oz (50g) balls Debbie Bliss baby cashmerino in Pale Blue (A).
- Small amounts of Mallard (B), Lime Green (C), Rose (D), Pale Pink (E) and White (F)
- Pair US 3 (3¼mm) knitting needles
- US 3 (3¼mm) circular knitting needle
- 2 small buttons
- 14 small blue beads and 40 small pink beads
- Sewing thread

GAUGE

25 sts and 34 rows to 4in square over st st using
US 3 (3¼mm) needles.

ABBREVIATIONS

See page 121.

CHART NOTE

When working from charts, read right side (k) rows
from right to left and wrong side (p) rows from left to
right. Strand yarn not in use loosely across wrong side
of work to keep fabric elastic.

BACK

With US 3 (3¼mm) needles and B, cast on
67(73:79) sts.
Beg with a k row, work 3 rows in st st.
Picot row P1, * yrn, p2tog; rep from * to end.
Change to C .
Work 2 rows in st st.
Change to A.
Cont in st st and work 6 rows.
Beg with a k row, work 13 rows in st st from chart 1,
working between lines for correct size and repeating
the 16 st patt rep.
Cont in A until back measures 6¾(8:9)in from picot
row, ending with a p row.
Shape armholes
Bind off 7(8:9) sts at beg of next 2 rows. 53(57:61) sts.
Cont straight until back measures 8¼(9½:10¾)in
from picot row, ending with a p row.

Back opening
Next row K25(27:29) sts, turn and work on these
sts for first side of back opening, leave rem sts on a
spare needle.
Next row Cast on 3 sts, k these sts, then p to end.
28(30:32) sts.
Next row K to end.
Next row K3, p to end.
Rep the last 2 rows until back measures 11(12½:14)in
from picot row, ending at armhole edge.
Shape shoulder
Next row Bind off 12(13:14) sts, k to end.
Next row K3, p to end.
Leave these 16(17:18) sts on a holder.
With right side facing, rejoin yarn to rem sts on spare
needle, k to end.
Next row P to last 3 sts, k3.
Next row K to end.
Rep the last 2 rows until back measures 9¾(11:12¼)in
from picot row, ending with a wrong side row.
Buttonhole row K1, k2tog, yf, k to end.
Work straight until back measures 11(12½:14)in from
picot row, ending at armhole edge.
Shape shoulder
Next row Bind off 12(13:14) sts, p to last 3 sts, k3.
Leave these 16(17:18) sts on a holder.

fair isle top

FRONT

Work as given for Back until front measures 9(10¼:11¾)in from picot row, ending with a p row.

Shape neck

Next row K19(20:21) sts, turn and work on these sts for first side of neck shaping, leave rem sts on a spare needle.

Dec 1 st at neck edge on every foll alt row until 12(13:14) sts rem.

Cont without further shaping until front measures same as Back to shoulder, ending at side edge.

Shape shoulder

Bind off.

With right side facing, slip center 15(17:19) sts onto a holder, rejoin yarn to rem sts, k to end.

Complete to match first side, reversing shaping.

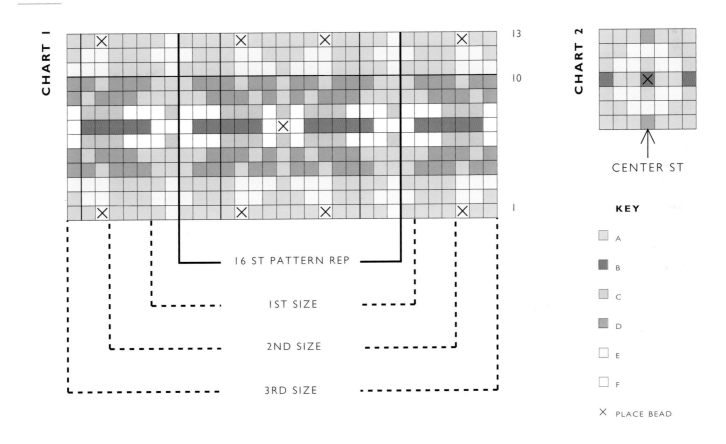

CHART 1

13

10

1

16 ST PATTERN REP

1ST SIZE

2ND SIZE

3RD SIZE

CHART 2

CENTER ST

KEY

☐ A

▨ B

☐ C

▨ D

☐ E

☐ F

✕ PLACE BEAD

SLEEVES

With US 3 (3¼mm) needles and B, cast on 49(55:61) sts.

Beg with a k row, work 3 rows in st st.

Picot row P1, * yrn, p2tog; rep from * to end.

Beg with a k row, work in st st throughout.

Change to C and work 2 rows.

Change to A and work 4 rows.

Work 7 rows in st st from chart 2, placing center st of chart on center st of row.

Cont in A only.

Next row P to end and inc 1 st in center of row. 50(56:62) sts.

Dec row K3, skpo, k to last 5 sts, k2tog, k3.

Work 5 rows in st st.

Rep the last 6 rows 3(4:5) times more and the dec row again. 40(44:48) sts.

Work 3 rows in st st.

Inc row K3, m1, k to last 3 sts, m1, k3.

Rep the last 4 rows 4(5:6) times more. 50(56:62) sts.

Cont straight until sleeve measures 7(8¼:9½)in from picot row, ending with a p row.

Mark each end of last row with a colored thread.

Work a further 6(8:8) rows.

Bind off.

NECKBAND

Join shoulder seams.

With right side facing, US 3 (3¼mm) circular needle and A, work k1, k2tog, yf, k13(14:15) from sts on left back holder, pick up and k20(20:21) sts down left front neck, k across 15(17:19) sts from front neck holder, pick up and k20(20:21) sts up right front neck to shoulder, then k across 16(17:18) sts from right back holder. 87(91:97) sts.

Cut yarn.

Change to E and keeping right side facing, k 1 row.

Now work back and forth in rows.

Next row (wrong side) Bind off 3 sts, p to last 3 sts, bind off these 3 sts.

Change to D.

K 1 row.

Picot row (wrong side) P1, * yrn, p2tog; rep from * to end.

Work 2 rows in st st.

Bind off.

TO FINISH

With center of bound off edge of sleeve to shoulder, sew sleeves into armholes with row ends above markers sewn to bound off sts at underarm. Join side and sleeve seams. Fold edges onto wrong side along picot row and slipstitch in place. Sew on buttons.

BEADS

Sew beads onto the garment where indicated on the charts, omitting beads where they would be incorporated into the side or sleeve seams.

fair isle top

bow-tied bolero

MEASUREMENTS

To fit ages	6–9	9–12	12–18	18–24	24–36	months

ACTUAL MEASUREMENTS

Chest	19	20	21¼	23½	25¼	in
Length to shoulder	6¾	7½	8¼	9	10	in
Sleeve length	3½	4¼	4¾	5½	6¼	in

MATERIALS

• 2(3:3:4:4) 1¾oz (50g) balls of Debbie Bliss baby cashmerino in Rose
• Pair each of US 2 (3mm) and US 3 (3¼mm) knitting needles
• Circular US 2 (3mm) knitting needle

GAUGE

25 sts and 34 rows to 4in square over st st using
US 3 (3¼mm) needles.

ABBREVIATIONS

See page 121.

BACK

With US 2 (3mm) needles, cast on 62(66:70:74:82) sts.
K 3 rows.
Change to US 3 (3¼mm) needles.
Beg with a k row, work 24(26:28:30:32) rows in st st.

Shape armholes
Bind off 3(3:3:3:4) sts at beg of next 2 rows.
Dec one st at each end of the next and 3(3:3:3:4) foll alt rows. 48(52:56:60:64) sts.
Cont in st st until back measures 6¾(7½:8¼:9:10)in from cast on edge, ending with a p row.

Shape shoulders
Bind off 13(14:15:16:17) sts at beg of next 2 rows.
Leave rem 22(24:26:28:30) sts on a holder.

LEFT FRONT

With US 2 (3mm) needles, cast on 93(99:105:111:123) sts.
K 3 rows.
Change to US 3 (3¼mm) needles.
Next row K to last 3 sts, m1, k3.
Next row K3, p to end.
Rep the last 2 rows 2(3:4:5:6) times more. 96(103:110:117:130) sts.
Next row K to last 32(37:42:47:56) sts, turn and leave these sts on a holder.
Next row Sl 1, p to end.
Next row K to last 10 sts, turn and leave these sts on a holder.
Next row Sl 1, p to end.
Next row K to last 8 sts, turn and leave these sts on a holder.
Next row Sl 1, p to end.

Next row K to last 6 sts, turn and leave these sts on a holder.
Next row Sl 1, p to end.
Next row K to last 4 sts, turn and leave these sts on a holder.
Next row Sl 1, p to end.
Next row K to last 2 sts, turn and leave these sts on a holder.
Next row Sl 1, p to end.
Next row K to last 2 sts, k2tog.
Next row P2tog, p to end.
Rep the last 2 rows twice more. 28(30:32:34:38) sts.

Shape armhole
Next row Bind off 3(3:3:3:4) sts, k to last 2 sts, k2tog.
Next row P to end.
Next row Skpo, k to last 2 sts, k2tog.
Next row P to end.
Rep the last 2 rows 3(3:3:3:4) times.
Keeping armhole edge straight, cont to dec at neck edge on every foll 4th row until 13(14:15:16:17) sts rem.
Cont straight until front measures same as Back to shoulder, ending at armhole edge.

Shape shoulder
Bind off.

RIGHT FRONT

With US 2 (3mm) needles, cast on 93(99:105:111:123) sts.
K 3 rows.
Change to US 3 (3¼mm) needles.
Next row K3, m1, k to end.
Next row P to last 3 sts, k3.

b o w - t i e d   b o l e r o

Rep the last 2 rows 2(3:4:5:6) times more.
96(103:110:117:130) sts.
Next row K32(37:42:47:56) sts, leave these sts on a holder, k to end.
Next row P to last st, sl 1.
Next row K10 sts, leave these sts on a holder, k to end.
Next row P to last st, sl 1.
Next row K8 sts, leave these sts on a holder, k to end.
Next row P to last st, sl 1.
Next row K6 sts, leave these sts on a holder, k to end.
Next row P to last st, sl 1.
Next row K4 sts, leave these sts on a holder, k to end.
Next row P to last st, sl 1.
Next row K2 sts, leave these sts on a holder, k to end.
Next row P to last st, sl 1.
Next row Skpo, k to end.
Next row P to last 2 sts, p2tog tbl.
Rep the last 2 rows twice more.
Next row Skpo, k to end. 27(29:31:33:37) sts.
Shape armhole
Next row Bind off 3(3:3:3:4) sts, p to end.
Next row Skpo, k to last 2 sts, k2tog.
Next row P to end.
Rep the last 2 rows 3(3:3:3:4) times.
Keeping armhole edge straight, cont to dec at neck edge on every foll 4th row until 13(14:15:16:17) sts rem.
Cont straight until front measures same as Back to shoulder, ending at armhole edge.
Shape shoulder
Bind off.

With US 2 (3mm) needles, cast on 38(40:44:48:52) sts.
K 3 rows.
Change to US 3 (3¼mm) needles.
Beg with a k row, work in st st and inc one st at each end of the 3rd and every foll 4th row until there are 50(54:60:66:74) sts.
Cont straight until sleeve measures 3½(4¼:4¾:5½:6¼)in from cast on edge, ending with a p row.
Bind off 3(3:3:3:4) sts at beg of next 2 rows.
Dec one st at each end of the next and 3(3:3:3:4) foll alt rows. 36(40:46:52:56) sts.
Bind off.

FRONT EDGING
Join shoulder seams.
With right side facing and US 2 (3mm) circular needle, slip 62(67:72:77:86) sts from right front holders onto needle, pick up and k27(30:33:36:40) sts up right front to shoulder, k across 22(24:26:28:30) sts at back neck, pick up and k27(30:33:36:40) sts down left front, then k across 62(67:72:77:86) sts on left front holders. 200(218:236:254:282) sts.
Working backwards and forwards, k 3 rows.
Bind off.

TO FINISH
Sew sleeves into armholes. Join side and sleeve seams.

beaded cardigan

MEASUREMENTS

To fit ages		12–18	18–24	24–36	months

ACTUAL MEASUREMENTS

Chest		24¾	26	27¼	in
Length to shoulder		11	12½	14¼	in
Sleeve length		7½	8¾	9½	in

MATERIALS

• 4(4:5) 1¾oz (50g) balls of Debbie Bliss baby cashmerino in Pale Blue
• Pair each of US 2 (3mm) and US 3 (3¼mm) knitting needles
• 7(7:8) buttons
• Approximately 1(1¼:1½)oz small glass beads with a silver core

25 sts and 34 rows to 4in square over st st using US 3 (3¼mm) needles.

ABBREVIATIONS
See page 121.

BACK
With US 3 (3¼mm) needles, cast on 81(85:89) sts.
Seed st row K1, * p1, k1; rep from * to end.
This row forms seed st.
Rep the last row 3 times more.
5th row (right side) [K1, p1] 2(3:4) times, * k3, p1, [k1, p1] 3 times; rep from * to last 7(9:11) sts, k3, [p1, k1] 2(3:4) times.
6th row P0(0:2), [k1, p1] 1(2:2) times, k1, * p5, k1, [p1, k1] twice; rep from * to last 8(10:12) sts, p5, k1, [p1, k1] 1(2:2) times, p0(0:2).
7th row K1(1:3), p1, k0(1:1), p0(1:1), k7, * p1, k1, p1, k7; rep from * to last 2(4:6) sts, p1, k1, p0(1:1), k0(1:3).
8th row P0(2:4), * k1, p9; rep from * to last 1(3:5) sts, k1, p0(2:4).
9th row K.
10th row P.
11th row K0(2:4), * p1, k9; rep from * to last 1(3:5) sts, p1, k0(2:4).

12th row P1(1:3), k1, p7, * k1, p1, k1, p7; rep from * to last 2(4:6) sts, [k1, p1] 1(2:2) times, p0(0:2).
13th row As 11th row.
14th row P.
15th row K5(7:9), * p1, k9; rep from * to last 6(8:10) sts, p1, k5(7:9).
16th row P4(6:8), * k1, p1, k1, p7; rep from * to last 7(9:11) sts, k1, p1, k1, p4(6:8).
17th row As 15th row.
The last 8 rows (10th to 17th patt rows) form the patt and are repeated.
Cont in patt until back measures 11(12½:14¼)in from cast on edge, ending with a wrong side row.
Shape shoulders
Bind off 23(24:25) sts at beg of next 2 rows.
Leave rem 35(37:39) sts on a spare needle.

beaded cardigan

LEFT FRONT

With US 3 (3¼mm) needles, cast on 43(45:47) sts.

Seed st row K1, * p1, k1; rep from * to end.

Rep the last row 3 times more.

5th row (right side) [K1, p1] 2(3:4) times, * k3, p1, [k1, p1] 3 times; rep from * to last 9 sts, k3, [p1, k1] 3 times.

6th row K1, [p1, k1] twice, * p5, k1, [p1, k1] twice; rep from * to last 8(10:12) sts, p5, k1, [p1, k1] 1(2:2) times, p0(0:2).

7th row K1(1:3), p1, k0(1:1), p0(1:1), k7, * p1, k1, p1, k7; rep from * to last 4 sts, [p1, k1] twice.

8th row K1, p1, * k1, p9; rep from * to last 1(3:5) sts, k1, p0(2:4).

9th row K to last 4 sts, [p1, k1] twice.

10th row K1, [p1, k1] twice, p to end.

11th row K0(2:4), * p1, k9; rep from * to last 13 sts, p1, k6, [p1, k1] 3 times.

12th row K1, [p1, k1] 3 times, p4, * k1, p1, k1, p7; rep from * to last 2(4:6) sts, [k1, p1] 1(2:2) times, p0(0:2).

13th row As 11th row.

14th row As 10th row.

15th row K5(7:9), * p1, k9; rep from * to last 8 sts, p1, k3, [p1, k1] twice.

16th row K1, p1, k1, p3, * k1, p1, k1, p7; rep from * to last 7(9:11) sts, k1, p1, k1, p4(6:8).

17th row As 15th row.

The last 8 rows (10th to 17th patt rows) form the patt and are repeated.

Cont in patt until left front measures 8¼(9¾:11½)in from cast on edge, ending with a wrong side row.

Shape neck

Next row Patt to last 8(9:10) sts, leave these sts on a holder.

Dec one st at neck edge on every row until 23(24:25) sts rem.

Cont straight until front measures same as Back to shoulder, ending at armhole edge.

Shape shoulder

Bind off.

Mark the position for 7(7:8) buttons, the first to come on the 5th row, the last just below the neck shaping, with the rem 5(5:6) evenly spaced between.

RIGHT FRONT

With US 3 (3¼mm) needles, cast on 43(45:47) sts.

Seed st row K1, * p1, k1; rep from * to end.

Rep the last row 3 times more.

Next row (buttonhole row) K1, p1, yon, p2tog, k1, p1, * k3, p1, [k1, p1] 3 times; rep from * to last 7(9:11) sts, k3, [p1, k1] 2(3:4) times.

6th row P0(0:2), [k1, p1] 1(2:2) times, k1, * p5, k1, [p1, k1] twice; rep from * to end.

7th row [K1, p1] twice, k7, * p1, k1, p1, k7; rep from * to last 2(4:6) sts, p1, k1, p0(1:1), k0(1:3).

8th row P0(2:4), * k1, p9; rep from * to last 3 sts, k1, p1, k1.

9th row [K1, p1] twice, k to end.

10th row P to last 5 sts, [k1, p1] twice, k1.

11th row [K1, p1] 3 times, k6, * p1, k9; rep from * to last 1(3:5) sts, p1, k0(2:4).

12th row P0(0:3), [p1, k1] 1(2:2) times, * p7, k1, p1, k1; rep from * to last 11 sts, p4, k1, [p1, k1] 3 times.

13th row As 11th row.

14th row As 10th row.

15th row [K1, p1] twice, k3, * p1, k9; rep from * to last 6(8:10) sts, p1, k5(7:9).

16th row P4(6:8), * k1, p1, k1, p7; rep from * to last 9 sts, k1, p1, k1, p3, k1, p1, k1.

17th row As 15th row.

The last 8 rows (10th to 17th patt rows) form the patt and are repeated.

Cont in patt working buttonholes on right side rows to match button markers, until right front measures 8¼(9¾:11½)in from cast on edge, ending with the same wrong side row as left front.

Shape neck

Next row Patt 8(9:10) sts, slip these sts onto a holder, patt to end.

Dec one st at neck edge on every row until 23(24:25) sts rem.

Cont straight until front measures same as Back to shoulder, ending at armhole edge.

Shape shoulder

Bind off.

beaded cardigan

SLEEVES

With US 3 (3¼mm) needles, cast on 35(37:39) sts.

1st and 3rd sizes only

Seed st row P1, * k1, p1; rep from * to end.

Rep the last row 3 times more.

2nd size only

Seed st row K1, * p1, k1; rep from * to end.

Rep the last row 3 times more.

All sizes

5th row (right side) P0(0:1), k0(1:1), p1, k3, * p1, [k1, p1] 3 times, k3; rep from * to last 1(2:3) sts, p1, k0(1:1), p0(0:1).

6th row P0(0:1), k0(1:1), p5, * k1, [p1, k1] twice, p5; rep from * to last 0(1:2) sts, k0(1:1), p0(0:1).

7th row P0(0:1), k6(7:7), * p1, k1, p1, k7; rep from * to last 9(10:11) sts, p1, k1, p1, k6(7:7), p0(0:1).

8th row P7(8:9), k1, * p9, k1; rep from * to last 7(8:9) sts, k7(8:9).

9th row K1, m1, k to last st, m1, k1.

10th row P.

11th row K8(9:10), * p1, k9; rep from * to last 9(10:11) sts, p1, k8(9:10).

12th row P7(8:9), * k1, p1, k1, p7; rep from * to last 0(1:2)sts, p0(1:2).

13th row K1, m1, k7(8:9), * p1, k9; rep from * to last 9(10:11) sts, p1, k7(8:9), m1, k1.

14th row P.

15th row K4(5:6), * p1, k9; rep from * to last 5(6:7) sts, p1, k4(5:6).

16th row P3(4:5), * k1, p1, k1, p7; rep from * to last 6(7:8) sts, k1, p1, k1, p3(4:5).

17th row K1, m1, k3(4:5), * p1, k9; rep from * to last 5(6:7) sts, p1, k3(4:5), m1, k1.

The last 8 rows set the position of the patt, cont in patt and inc one st at each end of every foll 4th row until there are 63(71:79) sts, taking all inc sts into patt.

Cont straight until sleeve measures 7½ (8¾:9½)in from cast on edge, ending with a wrong side row.

Bind off.

NECKBAND

Join shoulder seams.

With right side facing and US 2 (3mm) needles, slip 8(9:10) sts from right front neck holder onto a needle, pick up and k20 sts up right front neck, k35(37:39) sts from back neck holder, pick up and k20 sts down left front neck, patt across 8(9:10) sts from left front neck holder. 91(95:99) sts.

Work 5 rows in seed st.

Bind off in seed st.

TO FINISH

Matching center of bound off edge of sleeve to shoulder, sew on sleeves. Stitch one bead to the center of each tiny diamond, omitting diamonds that will be incorporated into the side and sleeve seams. Join side and sleeve seams. Sew on buttons.

sampler blanket

MEASUREMENTS
Approximately 24½ x 30in

MATERIALS
• Six 1¾oz (50g) balls of Debbie Bliss baby cashmerino in White (A)
• One 1¾oz (50g) ball in each of Indigo (B), Duck Egg (C) and Wedgwood (D)
• Pair of US 3 (3¼mm) knitting needles
• Large-eyed, blunt-pointed embroidery needle

GAUGE
25 sts and 34 rows to 4in square over st st using
US 3 (3¼mm) needles.

ABBREVIATIONS
See page 121.

CHART NOTES

To work from chart read 1st and every right side (k) row from right to left, 2nd and every wrong side (p) row from left to right.

Use separate lengths of yarn for each motif and wherever possible for the background in A between motifs. Twist yarns when changing colors to link areas. Work the area within the dotted outline containing the letters and numbers in plain stockinette stitch. Cross stitch the alphabet or use the letters and numbers to work a name and date after completing the knitting.

TO MAKE

With US 3 (3¼mm) needles and A, cast on 157 sts.

1st row (right side) P1, [k1, p1] to end.

2nd row K1, [p1, k1] to end.

3rd row K1, [p1, k1] to end.

4th row P1, [k1, p1] to end.

These 4 rows form double seed st.

Work 7 more rows, so ending with a right side row.

Next row (wrong side) Double seed st 11, k to last 11 sts, double seed st 11.

This row forms a ridge on the right side to outline the lower edge of the pattern area.

Next row (right side) Double seed st 11, p1, k133, p1, double seed st 11.

Next row Double seed st 11, k1, p133, k1, double seed st 11.

These 2 rows form st st with a single st in reverse st st and 11 sts in double seed st at each side.

Work 4 more rows.

Now work in patt from chart as folls:

1st row (right side) With A, patt 15, k127 sts of 1st row of chart, with A, patt 15.

2nd row With A, patt 15, p127 sts of 2nd row of chart, with A, patt 15.

These 2 rows set the position of the chart with 11 sts in double seed st and 4 sts in st st in A, worked at each side.

Cont in patt as set until all 227 chart rows have been worked.

Cont in A only.

Next row (wrong side) Double seed st 11, k1, p133, k1, double seed st 11.

Working center 133 sts in st st, work 4 more rows.

Next row (right side) Double seed st 11, p135, double seed st 11.

This last row forms a ridge to outline the top edge of the pattern area.

Work 10 rows in double seed st.

Bind off knitwise.

s a m p l e r   b l a n k e t

WORKING THE CROSS STITCH

The letters and numbers shown on the chart fit into an area 69 stitches by 106 rows. To work the complete alphabet as shown, use tacking thread to outline the stitches and rows indicated by the dotted line on the chart, then tack a base line for each row of letters. Use a blunt-pointed needle and work the cross stitch from the chart, placing each cross stitch over a knitted stitch, taking care to make all the top diagonals of the cross stitches lie in the same direction.

To cross stitch a name and date, plan your design on graph paper. The maximum area that lettering can comfortably be fitted into is 79 stitches by 110 rows. Mark this area on graph paper, then draw in dotted lines horizontally and vertically to cross at the center. Place an equal amount of letters at each side of the center vertical line and aim for no more than five or six letters on each line, with a maximum of six lines. Plan the lettering on the graph paper, adjusting the space between letters as necessary. Mark out the area to be worked on the blanket with tacking stitches, and tack guide lines for each row of letters and numbers before working the cross stitch from your chart.

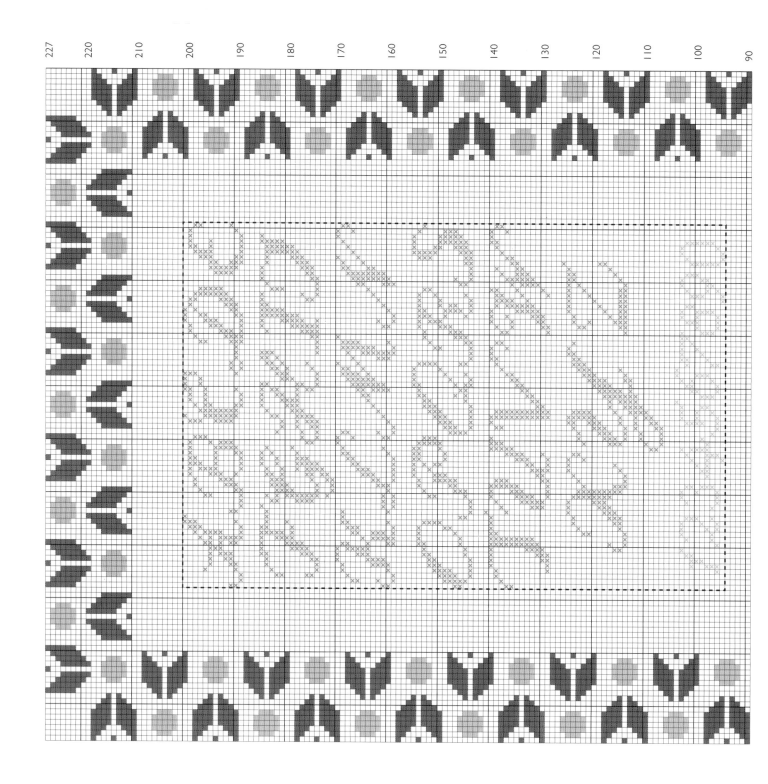

sampler blanket

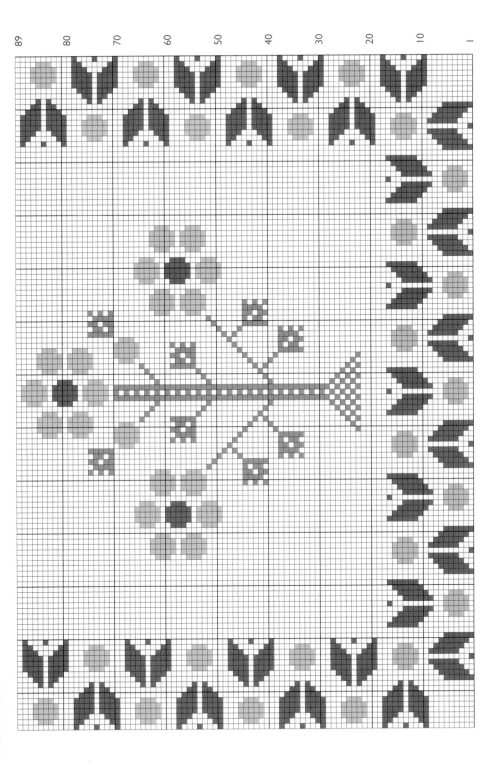

KEY

□ A

■ B

▨ C

▨ D

✕ CROSS STITCH IN C ON COMPLETION

✕ CROSS STITCH IN D ON COMPLETION

organza-edged cardigan

MEASUREMENTS

To fit ages	3–6	6–9	9–12	12–24	months

ACTUAL MEASUREMENTS

Chest	20	21¾	23½	25¼	in
Length to shoulder	10¼	11	13¼	14½	in
Sleeve length	6	6¾	7½	8¾	in

MATERIALS

• 3(3:4:4) 1¾oz (50g) balls of Debbie Bliss cotton cashmere double knitting in Grape

• Pair each of US 3 (3¼mm) and US 5 (3¾mm) knitting needles

• Approximately 1¾yd organza ribbon

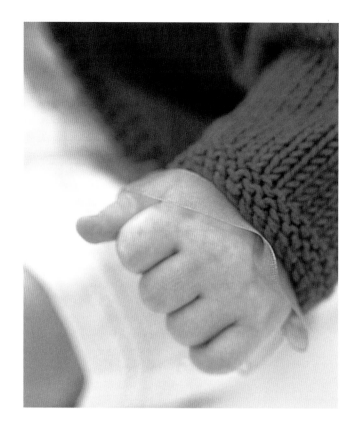

GAUGE

22 sts and 30 rows to 4in square over st st using
US 5 (3¾mm) needles.

ABBREVIATONS

See page 121.

BACK AND FRONTS

With US 3 (3¼mm) needles, cast on 59(63:69:73) sts.
K 3 rows.
Change to US 5 (3¾mm) needles.
Beg with a k row, work in st st until back measures
9¾(10½:13:14¼)in from cast on edge, ending with
a k row.
Next row P15(17:19:21), k29(29:31:31),
p15(17:19:21).
Next row K to end.
Next row P15(17:19:21), k29(29:31:31), p15(17:19:21).
Divide for fronts
Mark each end of last row with a colored thread.
Next row K17(19:21:23), turn and work on these sts
for right front, leave rem sts on a spare needle.
Next row K3, p to end.
Next row K to end.
Rep the last 2 rows once more and the first row again.
Next row K to last 3 sts, m1, k3.
Next row K3, p to end.
Next row K to end.
Next row K3, m1 purlwise, p to end.
Next row K to end.
Next row K3, p to end.
Cont in this way increasing one st inside garter st border
on every 3rd row until there are 25(27:30:32) sts.

Keeping 3 sts at front edge in garter st work straight
until the same number of rows have been worked in st
st as on Back to markers, ending with a p row.
Change to US 3 (3¼mm) needles.
P 3 rows.
Bind off purlwise.
With right side facing, rejoin yarn to rem sts on spare
needle, bind off next 25(25:27:27) sts, k to end.
Next row P to last 3 sts, k3.
Next row K to end.
Rep the last 2 rows once more and the first row again.
Next row K3, m1, k to end.

organza-edged cardigan

Next row P to last 3 sts, k3.

Next row K to end.

Next row P to last 3 sts, m1 purlwise, k3.

Next row K to end.

Next row P to last 3 sts, k3.

Cont in this way increasing one st inside garter st border on every 3rd row until there are 25(27:30:32) sts.

Keeping 3 sts at front edge in garter st work straight until the same number of rows have been worked in st st as on back to markers, ending with a p row.

Change to US 3 (3¼mm) needles.

P 3 rows.

Bind off purlwise.

SLEEVES

With US 3 (3¼mm) needles, cast on 35(37:39:43) sts.

K 3 rows.

Change to US 5 (3¾mm) needles.

Beg with a k row, work in st st, inc one st at each end of the 7th and every foll 4th row until there are 49(53:59:65) sts.

Cont straight until sleeve measures 6(6¾:7½:8¾)in from cast on edge, ending with a wrong side row.

Bind off.

TO FINISH

With center of bound off edge of sleeve to shoulder markers, sew on sleeves. Join side and sleeve seams.

RIBBON EDGING

Measure around the cuffs and the front/back neck edge, then cut the ribbon into three lengths allowing an extra 2¼in for each cuff and 8in for the neck. Run a line of long tacking stitches along one edge of each ribbon length, pull up slightly to gather and stitch to the inside of the cuffs, front and neck edges, distributing the soft gathers evenly.

hooded kaftan

MEASUREMENTS

To fit ages		3–6		6–12		12–18		18–24		months

ACTUAL MEASUREMENTS

Chest		20½		21¾		24		25¼		in
Length to shoulder		10¼		11¾		13½		14		in
Sleeve length		6		6¾		7½		8¾		in

MATERIALS

- 4(5:6:7) 1¾oz (50g) balls of Debbie Bliss cotton cashmere double knitting in Stone
- Pair each of US 3 (3¼mm) and US 5 (3¾mm) knitting needles
- Small amounts of embroidery threads
- Embroidery needle

GAUGE

22 sts and 30 rows to 4in square over st st using
US 5 (3¾mm) needles.

ABBREVIATIONS

See page 121.

BACK

With US 3 (3¼mm) needles, cast on 59(63:69:73) sts.
K 3 rows.
Change to US 5 (3¾mm) needles.
1st row (right side) K to end.
2nd row K2, p to last 2 sts, k2.
Rep the last 2 rows twice more.
Beg with a k row, work in st st until back measures
6(7:8:8¾)in from cast on edge, ending with a p row.
Shape armholes
Bind off 3(3:4:4) sts at beg of next 2 rows.
Dec one st at each end of the next and 1(2:2:3) foll alt
rows. 49(51:55:57) sts. **
Cont straight until back measures
10¼(11¾:13½:14½)in from cast on edge,
ending with a p row.
Shape shoulders
Bind off 10(11:12:13) sts at beg of next 2 rows.
Bind off rem 29(29:31:31) sts.

FRONT

Work as given for Back to **.
Cont straight until front measures 7(8¼:9½:10¾)in
from cast on edge, ending with a p row.
Front opening
Next row K23(24:26:27), turn and work on
these sts only for first side of front, leave rem sts
on a spare needle.
Work straight until front measures same as Back to
shoulder, ending at side edge.
Shape shoulder
Bind off 10(11:12:13) sts at beg of next row.
P 1 row.
Leave rem 13(13:14:14) sts on a spare needle.
With right side facing, rejoin yarn to rem sts, bind off
3 sts, k to end.
Work straight until front measures same as Back to
shoulder, ending at side edge.
Shape shoulder
Bind off 10(11:12:13) sts at beg of next row.
Do not cut yarn, leave sts on needle.

hooded kaftan

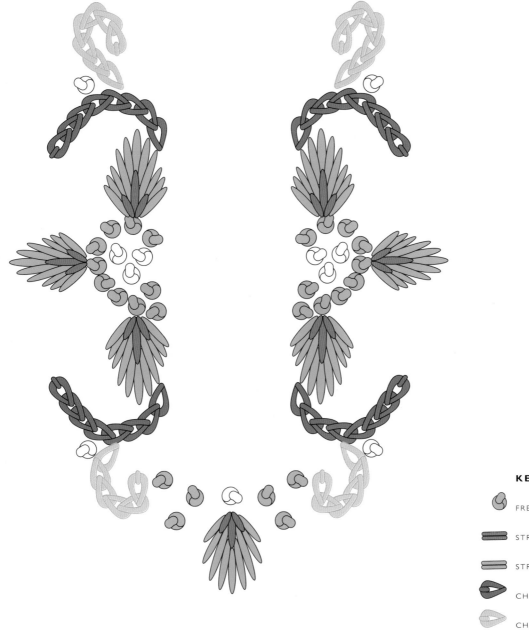

KEY

FRENCH KNOT IN ROSE

STRAIGHT STITCH IN FUCHSIA

STRAIGHT STITCH IN ROSE

CHAIN STITCH IN MALLARD

CHAIN STITCH IN PALE BLUE

FRENCH KNOT IN WHITE

HOOD

Join shoulder seams.

With right side facing and US 5 (3¾mm) needles, k across 13(13:14:14) sts from right front spare needle, cast on 41(41:44:44) sts, k across 13(13:14:14) sts from left front needle. 67(67:72:72) sts.

Cont in st st and work 3 rows.

Inc row K4, m1, k to last 4 sts, m1, k4.

Work 5 rows straight.

Rep the last 6 rows 9(10:11:12) times more.

Bind off.

SLEEVES

With US 3 (3¼mm) needles, cast on 35(37:43:45) sts.

K 3 rows.

Change to US 5 (3¾mm) needles.

Beg with a k row, work in st st, inc one st at each end of the 3rd and every foll 4th row until there are 53(59:69:75) sts.

Cont straight until sleeve measures 6(6¾:7½:8¾)in from cast on edge, ending with a wrong side row.

Shape top

Bind off 3(3:4:4) sts at beg of next 2 rows.

Dec one st at each end of the next and 1(2:2:3) foll alt rows. 43(47:55:59) sts.

Bind off.

FRONT EDGINGS

With right side facing and US 3 (3¼mm) needles, pick up and k70(78:86:92) sts along each front edge.

K 3 rows.

Bind off.

EMBROIDERY

Following the diagrams on page 101, work embroidery around the neck and sleeves edges.

TO FINISH

Sew sleeves into armholes. Join sleeve seams. Join side seams to top of opening. Join hood seam. Sew row ends of front edging to sts bound off at center front. Sew cast on edge of hood to bound off sts at back neck.

hooded kaftan

carrying bag

MEASUREMENTS

Approximately 16 x 30in

MATERIALS

- Eight 1¾oz (50g) balls Debbie Bliss cashmerino aran in Cream
- Pair of US 8 (5mm) knitting needles
- 1yd of 36-in wide fabric
- 1⅛ yd of ribbon
- Sewing thread and needle

GAUGE

18 sts and 32 rows to 4in square over seed stitch using US 8 (5mm) needles.

ABBREVIATIONS

See page 121.

TO MAKE

With US 8 (5mm) needles, cast on 137 sts.
Seed st row K1, [p1, k1] to end.
Work in seed st until bag measures 32in from cast on edge.
Bind off.

TO FINISH

Lay the knitted piece on top of the fabric, then adding ¾in all around, cut the fabric to size. With right sides together, fold the fabric in half. Matching the two shorter ends and taking a ¾in seam, stitch from the fold to the edges, across the bottom of the doubled fabric to form the base of the bag and continue the seam for 8¾in up the side. Press the seam open and continue to press the edges under around the remaining fabric, folding the top corners to neaten. Cut the ribbon into four pieces and stitch in pairs to each side of the bag. Fold the knitted piece in half matching the cast on and bound off edges. Stitch the lower edge and continue the seam for 8¾in along the side. Insert the knitted lining in the bag and slip stitch all around the open edges.

argyle cardigan

MEASUREMENTS

To fit ages	0–3	3–6	6–9	9–12	12–24	months

ACTUAL MEASUREMENTS

Chest	19	21	22¾	24¾	26¾	in
Length to shoulder	8½	9¾	10½	11½	13	in
Sleeve length	5	6	6¾	7½	8¾	in

MATERIALS

- 2(3:3:3:4) 1¾oz (50g) balls of Debbie Bliss baby cashmerino in Wedgwood (A)
- Small amounts in each of White (B) and Indigo (C)
- Pair each of US 2 (3mm) and US 3 (3¼mm) knitting needles
- US 3 (3¼mm) circular knitting needle
- 6(6:6:7:7) buttons

GAUGE

25 sts and 34 rows to 4in square over st st using
US 3 (3¼mm) needles.

ABBREVIATIONS

See page 121.

CHART NOTE

When working from chart read right side (k) rows
from right to left and wrong side (p) rows from left to
right. Work between lines for correct size, repeating
the 26 st pattern repeat. When working color motifs,
use separate small balls of each contrast yarn for each
area of color and twist yarns on wrong side when
changing color to avoid holes.

BACK AND FRONTS

With US 3 (3¼mm) circular needle and A, cast on
116(128:144:152:168) sts.
Work backwards and forwards in rows as follows:
1st row (right side) K3, * p2, k2; rep from * to last
5 sts, p2, k3.
2nd row P3, * k2, p2; rep from * to last 5 sts, k2, p3.
Rep these 2 rows twice more, increasing 3(4:1:6:3) sts
evenly across last row. 119(132:145:158:171) sts.
Beg with a k row work 4 rows in st st.
Cont in st st and work 11 rows from chart.
Cont in A only until back measures 5(6:6¼:6¾:7½)in
from cast on edge, ending with a p row.
Divide for back and fronts
Next row K26(30:32:35:38), leave these sts on a
holder for right front, bind off next 6(6:8:8:10) sts, k
until there are 55(60:65:72:75) sts on needle, leave
these sts on a holder for back, bind off next
6(6:8:8:10) sts, k to end.
Cont on last set of 26(30:32:35:38) sts only for
left front.
Dec one st at armhole edge on 3(4:4:5:5) foll alt rows.
23(26:28:30:33) sts.
Cont straight until work measures 7(8:8¾:9:10¾)in
from cast on edge, ending with a p row.
Shape neck
Next row K to last 4(5:5:5:6) sts, turn and leave these
sts on a holder.
Dec one st at neck edge on every row until
13(14:15:16:17) sts rem.
Cont straight until work measures
8¾(9¾:10¾:11½:13)in from cast on edge, ending at
armhole edge.

argyle cardigan

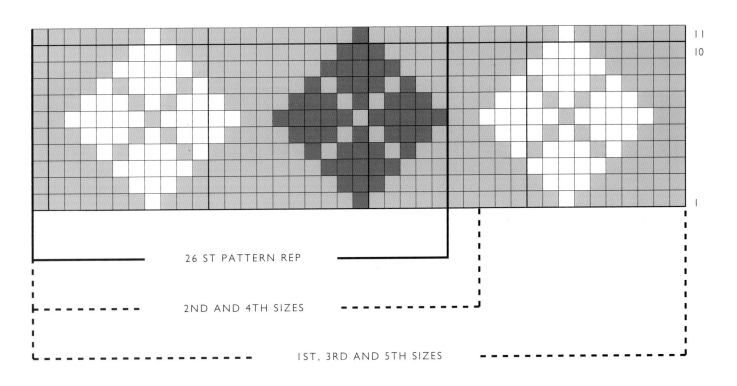

11
10
1

26 ST PATTERN REP

2ND AND 4TH SIZES

1ST, 3RD AND 5TH SIZES

KEY

A

B

C

Shape shoulder

Bind off.

With wrong side facing, rejoin yarn to center 55(60:65:72:75) sts for back, p to end.

Shape armholes

Dec one st at each end of next row and 2(3:3:4:4) foll alt rows. 49(52:57:62:65) sts.

Cont straight until back measures same as left front to shoulder, ending with a wrong side row.

Shape shoulders

Bind off 13(14:15:16:17) sts at beg of next 2 rows.

Leave rem 23(24:27:30:31) sts on a holder.

With wrong side facing, work across last set of 26(30:32:35:38) sts for right front.

Dec one st at armhole edge on next row and 2(3:3:4:4) foll alt rows. 23(26:28:30:33) sts.

Cont straight until work measures 7(8:8¾:9:10¾)in from cast on edge, ending with a p row.

Shape neck

Next row K4(5:5:5:6) sts, leave these sts on a holder, k to end.

Dec one st at neck edge on every row until 13(14:15:16:17) sts rem.

Cont straight until work measures 8¾(9¾:10¾:11½:13)in from cast on edge, ending at armhole edge.

Shape shoulder

Bind off.

SLEEVES

With US 2 (3mm) needles and A, cast on 34(34:38:38:42) sts.

1st row (right side) K2, * p2, k2; rep from * to end.

2nd row P2, * k2, p2; rep from * to end.

Change to US 3 (3¼mm) needles.

Rep these last 2 rows once more and inc 2 sts evenly across last row. 36(36:40:40:44) sts.

Beg with a k row, work in st st and inc one st at each end of the 3rd and every foll 4th row until there are 52(56:62:68:76) sts.

Cont straight until sleeve measures 5¼(6:6¾:7½:8¾)in from cast on edge, ending with a p row.

Bind off 4(4:5:5:6) sts at beg of next 2 rows.

Dec one st at each end of the next row and 2(3:3:4:4) foll alt rows. 38(40:44:48:54) sts.

Bind off.

argyle cardigan

NECKBAND

Join shoulder seams.

With right side facing, US 2 (3mm) needles and A, slip 4(5:5:5:6) sts from right front holder onto a needle, pick up and k16(16:17:17:18) sts up right front neck to shoulder, k across 23(24:27:30:31) sts of back neck and inc 1(2:1:2:1) sts evenly, pick up and k16(16:17:17:18) sts down left front neck, then k4(5:5:5:6) sts from left front neck holder. 64(68:72:76:80) sts.

Beg with a 2nd row, work 5 rows in rib as given for Back and Fronts.

Bind off in rib.

BUTTON BAND

With right side facing, US 2 (3mm) needles and A, pick up and k54(58:66:70:78) sts along left front edge.

Beg with a 2nd row, work 5 rows in rib as given for Sleeves.

Bind off in rib.

BUTTONHOLE BAND

With right side facing, US 2 (3mm) needles and A, pick up and k54(58:66:70:78) sts along right front edge.

Beg with a 2nd row, work one row in rib as given for Sleeves.

Buttonhole row (right side) Rib 3(3:4:4:2), [rib 2 tog, yf, rib 7(8:9:8:10) sts] 5(5:5:6:6) times, rib 2 tog, yf, rib 4(3:5:4:2).

Rib 2 rows.

Bind off in rib.

TO FINISH

Join sleeve seams. Sew sleeves into armholes.

Sew on buttons.

argyle
pullover

MEASUREMENTS

To fit ages		0–3		3–6		6–9		9–12		12–24		months

ACTUAL MEASUREMENTS

Chest		17¾		19¾		21		22¾		24¾		in
Length to shoulder		8¼		9½		10¼		11		12½		in

MATERIALS

- 2(2:3:3:3) 1¾oz (50g) balls of Debbie Bliss baby cashmerino in Wedgwood (A)
- Small amounts in each of White (B) and Indigo (C)
- Pair each of US 2 (3mm) and US 3 (3¼mm) knitting needles
- US 2 (3mm) circular knitting needle
- One small button

GAUGE

25 sts and 34 rows to 4in square over st st using
US 3 (3¼mm) needles.

ABBREVIATIONS

See page 121.

CHART NOTE

Use separate small balls of contrast yarn for each
motif and twist yarns at color change to avoid holes.
Work between lines for correct size, repeating the
26 st pattern repeat.

BACK

With US 2 (3mm) needles and A, cast on
58(62:66:74:78) sts.

1st row K2, * p2, k2; rep from * to end.

2nd row P2, * k2, p2; rep from * to end.

Rep the last 2 rows once more, and inc 1(3:3:1:3) sts
evenly across last row. 59(65:69:75:81) sts.

Change to US 3 (3¼mm) needles.

Beg with a k row, work 4 rows in st st.

Work 11 rows in st st from chart.

Cont in st st and A and work until back measures
4¼(5:5½:6:7)in from cast on edge, ending with a p row.

Shape armholes

Bind off 3(4:4:5:5) sts at beg of next 2 rows.

Dec one st at each end of the next and 3(3:4:4:5) foll
alt rows. 45(49:51:55:59) sts. **

Cont in st st until back measures 6(6¾:7½:8¾:10¼)in
from cast on edge, ending with a p row.

Back neck opening

1st row K23(25:26:28:30) sts, turn and work on these

sts for first side of neck shaping, leave rem sts on a
spare needle.

2nd row K2, p to end.

3rd row K to end.

Rep the last 2 rows until back measures
7½(8¾:9½:10¼:11¾)in from cast on edge, ending
with a wrong side row.

Shape neck

Next row K15(16:17:18:19) sts, turn, leave rem
8(9:9:10:11) sts on a safety pin.

Dec 1 st at neck edge on next 4 rows.

11(12:13:14:15) sts.

Work 3 rows in st st.

Bind off for shoulder.

With right side facing, rejoin yarn to sts on spare
needle, cast on one st, k to end.

2nd row P to last 2 sts, k2.

3rd row K to end.

Rep the last 2 rows until back measures
7½(8¾:9½:10¼:11¾)in from cast on edge, ending
with a k row.

Shape neck

Next row P15(16:17:18:19) sts, turn, leave rem
8(9:9:10:11) sts on a safety pin.

Dec 1 st at neck edge on next 4 rows.

11(12:13:14:15) sts.

Work 2 rows in st st.

Bind off for shoulder.

argyle pullover

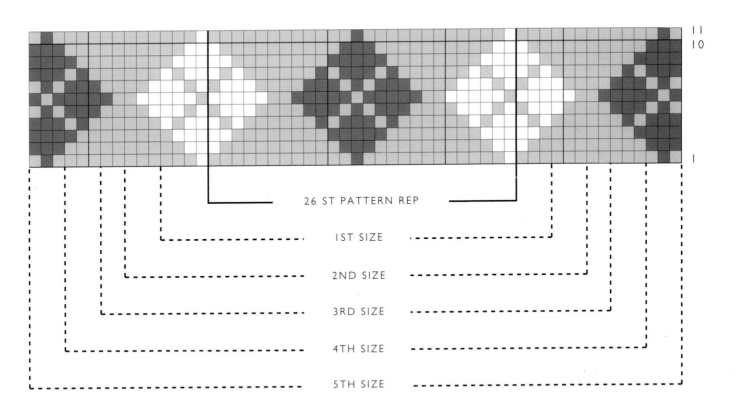

11
10

26 ST PATTERN REP

1ST SIZE

2ND SIZE

3RD SIZE

4TH SIZE

5TH SIZE

KEY

A

B

C

FRONT

Work as given for Back to **.

Cont in st st until front measures 6(7:8:8¼:9¾)in from cast on edge, ending with a p row.

Shape neck

Next row K17(18:19:20:21) sts, turn and work on these sts for first side of front neck, leave rem sts on a spare needle.

Dec 1 st at neck edge on next and every foll alt row until 11(12:13:14:15) sts rem.

Work straight until front measures same as Back to shoulder, ending with a p row.

Bind off.

With right side facing, slip center 11(13:13:15:17) sts onto a holder, rejoin yarn to rem sts on spare needle, k to end.

Complete to match first side of neck, reversing shaping.

NECKBAND

Join shoulder seams.

With right side facing, US 2 (3mm) circular needle and A, slip 8(9:9:10:11) sts from left back onto needle. pick up and k8 sts up left back neck, 15(15:15:17:17) sts down left side of front neck, k across 11(13:13:15:17) sts from front neck holder, pick up and k15(15:15:17:17) sts up right side of front neck, 9 sts down right back neck, k across 8(9:9:10:11) sts from back neck holder. 74(78:78:86:90) sts.

1st row P2, * k2, p2; rep from * to end.

2nd row K2, * p2, k2; rep from * to end.

Rep the last 2 rows once more.

Bind off in rib

ARMBANDS

With right side facing, US 2 (3mm) needles and A, pick up and k62(70:74:78:86) sts.

Work 4 rows in rib as given for Back.

Bind off in rib.

TO FINISH

Join side and armband seams. Make a button loop on left back neckband. Sew on button.

argyle pullover

picture index

8 Eyelet vest.
To fit ages 6–12, 12–18, 18–24, 24–36 months

12 Garter-stitch blanket.

14 Ribbed jacket.
To fit ages 0–3, 3–6, 6–9, 9–12, 12–24 months

18 Hooded sweater.
To fit ages 0–3, 3–6, 6–9, 9–12, 12–24 months

22 Embroidered kimono. To fit ages 3–6, 6–12, 12–18 months

28 Ribbon-edged cardigan. To fit ages 0–3, 3–6, 6–9, 9–12, 12–24 months

32 Rabbit.

36 Alphabet sweater.
To fit ages 3, 6, 12, 24 months

42 Check and cross-stitch jacket. To fit ages 6, 18, 24 months

48 Ribbon-tied dress.
To fit ages 3–6, 6–12, 12–18, 18–24 months

52 Shawl.

56 Picot dress and bag. To fit ages 3–6, 9–12, 12–18, 18–24 months

62 Velvet-edged jacket. To fit ages 0–3, 3–6, 6–9, 9–12, 12–24 months

68 Fair isle top. To fit ages 6–12, 12–18, 18–24 months

74 Bow-tied bolero. To fit ages 6–9, 9–12, 12–18, 18–24, 24–36 months

78 Beaded cardigan. To fit ages 12–18, 18–24, 24–36 months

86 Sampler blanket.

92 Organza-edged cardigan. To fit ages 3–6, 6–9, 9–12, 12–24 months

98 Hooded kaftan. To fit ages 3–6, 6–12, 12–18, 18–24 months

104 Carrying bag.

106 Argyle cardigan. To fit ages 0–3, 3–6, 6–9, 9–12, 12–24 months

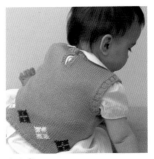

112 Argyle pullover. To fit ages 0–3, 3–6, 6–9, 9–12, 12–24 months

basic information

KNITTING ABBREVIATIONS

alt	alternate		pfb	purl into front and back of next st
beg	beginning		psso	pass slipped st over
cont	continue		rem	remaining
dec	decrease		rep	repeat
foll	following		skpo	slip 1, knit 1, pass slipped stitch over
inc	increase		sl	slip
k	knit		st(s)	stitch(es)
kfb	knit into front and back of next st		st st	stockinette stitch
m1	make one by picking up the loop lying between st just worked and next st and working into back of it		tbl	through back loop
			tog	together
			yf	yarn forward
patt	pattern		yon	yarn over needle
p	purl		yrn	yarn round needle

READING PATTERN INSTRUCTIONS

Figures for larger sizes are given in round ( ) brackets. Where only one figure appears this means that it applies to all the sizes. Work the figures given in square [ ] brackets the number of times quoted afterwards. Where 0 appears no stitches or rows are worked for this size.

The quantities of yarn stated in the pattern are based on the yarn amounts used by the knitter of the original garment. Yarn amounts therefore should be considered approximate as a slight variation in gauge can make the difference between using fewer or more balls or hanks than that stated. My patterns quote the actual chest measurements of the garment and not the child, check these measurements first as you may wish to make a smaller or larger garment for the age of the child.

GAUGE

Gauge is one of the most important aspects of hand knitting. Gauge is the number of stitches and rows per inch that should be obtained using the same yarn, needles and stitch as the pattern requires and will always be quoted at the beginning of a knitting pattern. A variation of stitches and rows over a certain measurement can make the difference between a smaller or larger garment than the size that you are knitting, a tighter fabric that is stiff and uncomfortable to wear or a looser one that is unstable and stretches. A garment has been

designed with the proportions very much in mind; if you have a different stitch gauge giving a wider or narrower width, but the length of the design is worked in measurement rather than rows, you will have a different shaped garment than the original design.

Always make a gauge square before you start the garment. Knit a sample approximately 5-in square using the needles and yarns quoted in the gauge note at the beginning of the pattern. Smooth out the finished square on a flat surface and leave it to relax for a while. To check the stitch gauge, place a tape measure or ruler horizontally on the sample and mark out 4in with pins. Count the number of stitches within the pins. To check the row gauge, place the tape measure vertically and mark out 4in with pins. Count the rows within the pins. If the number of stitches and rows is greater than that quoted it means your gauge is tighter and you need to use larger needles to create bigger stitches. If there are fewer stitches and rows, try a smaller needle to make smaller stitches. If you are only able to obtain either the correct stitch or row gauge, it is the stitch gauge that is the most important to get right, as often patterns are calculated in measurements rather than rows.

CARE OF GARMENTS

Always check the label for washing instructions. All the yarns used in this book are machine-washable, but with small garments like these it does not take much effort to handwash them, which I always prefer. Before washing make a note of the measurement, and

basic information

after washing dry the garment flat on a towel, patting it back into the shape if excess moisture is making it stretch slightly. Take care not to wring or rub the fabric and do not be tempted to dry it quickly with direct heat, such as a radiator.

YARN

Do check dye lot numbers when you are buying your yarn. Yarns are dyed in batches, and the color can vary between one lot and another. Buy an extra ball if you sometimes use more balls then the amount quoted in the pattern; you may find that if you go back to your retailer later to buy extra, it is no longer the same dye lot and there will be a variation in the shade, which although you can't see it in the ball, really shows up when knitted.

When buying yarn always try to buy the yarn that I have used in the pattern, as I will have designed the garment specifically with that yarn in mind. It may be because a particular yarn, such as a cotton, shows a subtle stitch, such as seed stitch, beautifully, and this will be lost if an inferior yarn is substituted. A hooded top in a cashmere mix is soft and snugly, but in a harder yarn it could be rough against a baby's skin.

If, however, you do decide to use a substitute yarn, always make sure that you can obtain the same gauge and where possible choose the same fiber content. Check the yardage on the ball band and if there are fewer yards in the ball than in the original yarn, you may need to buy extra balls.

The following information is a description of my yarns that have been used in this book and a guide to their weight and yardage.

■ DEBBIE BLISS CASHMERINO ARAN.
A 55% merino wool, 33% microfiber and 12% cashmere mix. Approx. 98½yds/1¾oz (90m/50g) ball.

■ DEBBIE BLISS BABY CASHMERINO.
The same luxury mix as above, but a lightweight yarn, between a 4ply and a double knitting. Approx. 136¾yds/1¾oz (125m/50g) ball.

■ DEBBIE BLISS COTTON CASHMERE.
85% cotton, 15% cashmere, in a double knitting weight. Approx. 104yds/1¾oz (95m/50g) ball.

SUPPLIERS

For suppliers of Debbie Bliss yarns please contact:

USA
Knitting Fever Inc.
P.O. Box 502
Roosevelt, New York 11575
Tel: (516) 546 3600
Fax: (516) 546 6871
www.knittingfever.com

Canada
Diamond Yarns Ltd, 155 Martin
Ross Avenue, Unit 3, Toronto,
Ontario M3J 2L9
Tel: 001 416 736 6111
www.diamondyarn.com

Mexico
Red Color, S.A. DE CV. San
Antonio 105, Col. Santa Maria,
Monterrey, N.L. 64650
Tel: +52 818 173 3700
e-mail: Abremer@starsoft.co.mx

Japan
Eisaku Noro & Co Ltd., 55
Shimoda Ohibino Azaichou,
Ichinomita Aichi, 4910105.
Tel: +81 52 203 5100
www.eisakunoro.com

UK
Designer Yarns Ltd, Units 8-10
Newbridge Industrial Estate, Pitt
Street, Keighley, W. Yorkshire,
BD21 4PQ
Tel: +44 (0)1535 664222
Fax: +44 (01535) 664333
www.designeryarns.uk.com
e-mail: jane@designeryarns.uk.com

Germany/Austria/Switzerland
Designer Yarns, Handelsagentur
Klaus Koch, Mauritius Str. 130
50226 Frechen.
Tel: +49 2234 205453
Fax: +49 2234 205456
www.designeryarns.de

France
Elle Tricote, 8 Rue du Coq,
(Petit France) 67000 Strasbourg.
Tel: +33 (0)388 230313
www.elletricote.com.fr

Spain
Oyambre, Pau Claris 145, 08009
Barcelona
Tel: +34 934 872672
e-mail:
oyambre@oyambreonline.com

Belgium/Holland
Pavan, Meerlaanstraat 73,
Oostrezele 9860
Tel: +32 9221 8594
Fax +32 9221 5662
e-mail: pavan@pandora.be

Sweden
Hamilton Design, Långgatan 20,
SE-64730, Mariefred.
Tel/fax: +46 (0)159 12006
www.hamiltondesign.biz

Australia
Sunspun, 185 Canterbury Road,
Canterbury VIC 3126
Tel: +61 (0)3 9830 1609
e-mail: shop@sunspun.com.au

Jo Sharp Pty Ltd., P.O. Box 1018,
Fremantle, WA 6959
Tel: +61 08 9430 9699
e-mail: yarn@josharp.com.au

Denmark
Strikkeboden, Krystalgade 16, 1172
Copenhagen K
Tel: +45 4583 0127
e-mail: jens.toersleff@get2net.dk

basic information

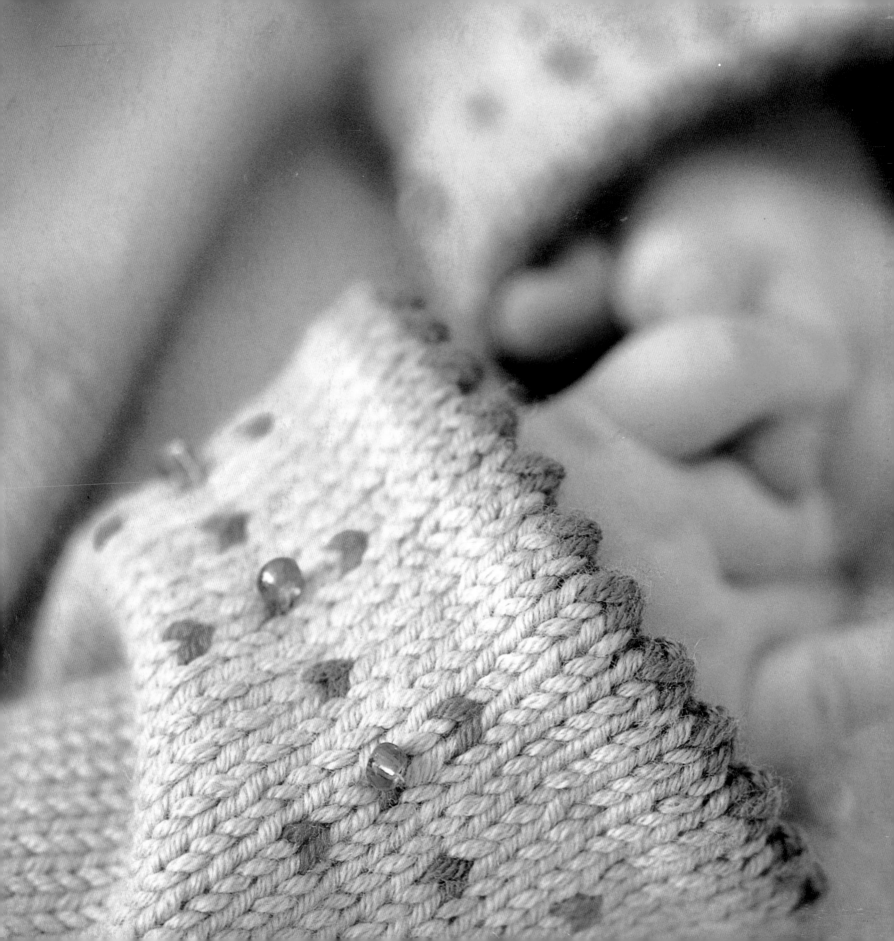

ACKNOWLEDGEMENTS

This book would not have been possible without the invaluable collaboration of the following:

Rosy Tucker, for pattern checking and creative contribution.

Penny Hill for pattern compiling and checking.

Melody Griffiths for her design involvement.

Sandra Lousada for her beautiful photography and her assistants, Anne, Bridget and Nicola.

Sammie Bell for the lovely styling.

Kate Haxell for being a great editor and Elvis for being a great dog.

Marie Clayton and Colin Ziegler for making it happen.

Roger Hammond@Blue Gum for the great book design.

Luise Roberts for the charts and artwork.

The brilliant knitters who work to impossible deadlines; Brenda Bostock, Cynthia Brent, Jill Borley, Sally Buss, Pat Church, Jacqui Dunt, Penny Hill, Shirley Kennet, Janet Kopinski, Maisie Lawrence, Gwen Radford, Jean Trehane and Frances Wallace.

The models, Ella, Afia, Poppy, Oliver, Charlotte, Isabelle, Sam, Amira, Wilf, Iris and Simah.

My wonderful agent, Heather Jeeves.

The knitters, retailers and distributors who support my yarns and books.

The day bed used in some of the photographs is from www.bumpstuff.com